Series/Number 07-107

CHAOS AND CATASTROPHE THEORIES

COURTNEY BROWN
Emory University

SAGE PUBLICATIONS
International Educational and Professional Publisher
Thousand Oaks   London   New Delhi

For information address:

SAGE Publications, Inc.
2455 Teller Road
Thousand Oaks, California 91320
E-mail: order@sagepub.com

SAGE Publications Ltd.
6 Bonhill Street
London EC2A 4PU
United Kingdom

SAGE Publications India Pvt. Ltd.
M-32 Market
Greater Kailash I
New Delhi 110 048 India

Printed in the United States of America

Library of Congress Cataloging-in-Publication Data

Brown, Courtney, 1952-
    Chaos and catastrophe theories / Courtney Brown.
        p. cm. — (Sage university papers series. Quantitative
applications in the social sciences; no. 07-107)
    Includes bibliographical references (pp. 75-76).
    ISBN 0-8039-5847-1 (pbk.: alk. paper)
    1. Chaotic behavior in systems.   2. Catastrophes (Mathematics)
I. Title.   II. Series.
Q172.5.C45B76   1995
300′.1′1385—dc20   95-9072

95 96 97 98 99 10 9 8 7 6 5 4 3 2 1

Sage Project Editor: Susan McElroy

When citing a university paper, please use the proper form. Remember to cite the current Sage University Paper series title and include the paper number. One of the following formats can be adapted (depending on the style manual used):

(1) BROWN, C. (1995) *Chaos and Catastrophe Theories.* Sage University Paper series on Quantitative Applications in the Social Sciences, 07-107. Thousand Oaks, CA: Sage.

OR

(2) Brown, C. (1995). *Chaos and catastrophe theories* (Sage University Paper series on Quantitative Applications in the Social Sciences, series no. 07-107). Thousand Oaks, CA: Sage.

CONTENTS

SERIES EDITOR'S INTRODUCTION

Courtney Brown takes us on a tour of major frontiers in social science—chaos and catastrophe theories. The tour is quite pleasant, for he makes the sophisticated mathematical and computational requirements readily understandable. The organization of the monograph is a marvel of simplicity, all the more so given the potential complexity of the material. Part One answers three fundamental questions: What is chaos? How do you measure it? How are the models estimated? Part Two also asks three fundamental questions: What is catastrophe? How do you measure it? How are the models estimated?

In social science faculty lounges these days, there is much loose talk about chaos and catastrophe. The ideas are all the fashion, but they are often poorly understood. Professor Brown clarifies things. Chaos is determined behavior that appears random. Catastrophe occurs when there is an abrupt major change in one variable as a result of a small change in something else. Chaos and catastrophe theories are joined, in that they are based on deterministic nonlinear dynamic models. Both continuous and discrete time models are included.

A chaotic process has an irregular cycle. Take a simple example. A person repeatedly buys gasoline for his or her car but does so at different times. Chaos is unpredictable and is so because of its extreme responsiveness to initial conditions. There are different ways to test a time series for chaos, such as Fourier analysis, or graphically. Good use is made of the graphs in diagnosis, because chaos leaves telltale markings. Quantitative measures of chaos include Lyapunov exponents and the spatial correlation test. Estimation of a chaotic system proceeds from nonlinear least squares methods. As with almost all optimization methods, it is especially important to ensure that the set of start values have not led to some local maximum. Also, great care must be taken that the time series observations are close enough together, or estimation may not be feasible.

In catastrophe theory, a "bifurcation" is a transforming event, brought about by an "attractor" changing after a parameter value change. As Professor Brown emphasizes, catastrophe theory should be developed from theories of society, not theories of mathematics. He notes that the most elementary catastrophe model—the "fold" model—asks for only a squared primary variable and additional input like a control parameter. Further, certain values of the control parameter can be created by two or more values of an X, a necessary condition for catastrophe. Estimation for catastrophe models goes forward as with chaos models, if there is one unit observed repeatedly over time. However, the more common social science situation, with many units but not many observations, requires different estimation, essentially in computation of goodness-of-fit measures. As an example, Professor Brown estimates a nonlinear system of equations that captures the possibility of catastrophe, utilizing 1980 survey data on President Carter's failed reelection campaign.

For those who have read *Dynamic Modeling* (Huckfeldt, Kohfeld, & Likens; No. 27 in this series), this effort is a good next step. Application of these theories is new. Few catastrophe models, and no chaos models, have actually been estimated on social science data. Perhaps the reader, after Professor Brown's artful explication of technique, will help change that report.

—*Michael S. Lewis-Beck*
Series Editor

CHAOS AND CATASTROPHE THEORIES

COURTNEY BROWN
Emory University

1. WORKING WITH
DETERMINISTIC MATHEMATICAL MODELS

Chaos and catastrophe theories are among the most interesting recent developments in nonlinear modeling, and both have captured the interests of scientists in many disciplines. It is only natural that social scientists should be concerned with these theories. Linear statistical models have proven very useful in a great deal of social scientific empirical analyses, as is evidenced by how widely these models have been used for a number of decades. However, there is no apparent reason, intuitive or otherwise, as to why human behavior should be more linear than the behavior of other things, living and nonliving. Thus an intellectual movement toward non-linear models is an appropriate evolutionary movement in social scientific thinking, if for no other reason than to expand our paradigmatic boundaries by encouraging greater flexibility in our algebraic specifications of all aspects of human life.

More specifically, chaos and catastrophe theories per se address behavioral phenomena that are consequences of two general types of nonlinear dynamic behavior. In the most elementary of behavioral terms, chaotic phenomena are a class of deterministic processes that seem to mimic random or stochastic dynamics. Catastrophe phenomena, on the other hand, are a class of dynamic processes that exhibit a sudden and large scale change in at least one variable in correspondence with relatively small changes in other variables or, in some cases, parameters.

This chapter explains the basic differences between deterministic models and probabilistic models, as well as why deterministic models are used with chaos and catastrophe theories. Also, an effort is made to explain why there is no great loss in abandoning probabilistic mathematics in this regard (see also Huckfeldt, Kohfeld, & Likens, 1982). More specifically, the chapter seeks to dispel potential misconceptions that could seduce some

1

readers into thinking that deterministic models may be inferior to stochastic models. Because the vast majority of empirical investigations in the social sciences currently utilize probabilistic models, this chapter is crucial to those researchers who want to begin or expand their own investigations into highly nonlinear algebraic specifications and who may wonder why the probabilistic approach is nearly useless in this setting.

To establish an overview of the relevant terrain, I present a typology of models that includes five categories and follows organizational suggestions offered by May (1974). The categories are (a) deterministic continuous time models, (b) deterministic discrete time models, (c) probabilistic continuous time models, (d) probabilistic discrete time models, and (e) models with randomly fluctuating parameters. This monograph explores models that fall within the first two categories, although the text includes a brief discussion of the last category (e) in relation to conditioned parameter estimation for chaos and catastrophe specifications.

Using May's terminology, the first general class of models is of the deterministic continuous time variety and is referenced here as Model I. Because exponential growth is among the simplest of dynamic processes, it is used heuristically in this presentation across all model categories. Thus we have

Model I: $$\frac{dN}{dt} = rN(t), \qquad (1.1)$$

where the analytical solution to this equation is the familiar form

$$N(t) = N_0 e^{rt} \qquad (1.2)$$

in which the population at any time t is a function of the growth parameter r and the initial population size N_0.

Social scientists often find it convenient to model behavioral phenomena using discrete mathematics. One reason for this is that all measurement of all phenomena are taken at discrete points in time, regardless of the dynamic structure of the underlying processes of change. For example, major census reports often appear in many countries every ten years, although population change may be more or less continuous. However, substantive reasons also apply for the use of discrete time models in many instances, such as when conducting investigations of electoral behavior in which voting occurs at regular intervals, or when a social phenomenon is structured longitudinally with respect to separate generations.

With discrete time models, the period of time between successive events is usually fixed according to the event calendar rather than via chronological measures (e.g., days, years, etc.), thereby simplifying the identification of time. The discrete time model that is analogous to Equation 1.1 is

$$\Delta N(t) = rN(t), \tag{1.3}$$

or, more commonly,

Model II: $$N(t + 1) = (1 + r)N(t). \tag{1.4}$$

The analytical solution to Model II is

$$N(t) = N_0(1 + r)^t,$$

where N_0 is again the initial population size.

The comparable stochastic version of Model I (i.e., in continuous time) is more involved than its deterministic counterpart. An exceptionally clear description of the mathematics involved can be obtained in Bailey (1964, pp. 67-69 and 84-87; but see also Bartlett, 1966, p. 74; Feller, 1968, pp. 448-451; and May, 1974, pp. 31-32). The process requires the assignment of a probability of an event in an infinitesimal period of time. However, it is useful to begin the exposition of this model with a more general statement addressing any fixed period of time, Δt, before taking the limit. Because the probability of one event occurring in such a time interval is $r\Delta t$ and the probability of no event in the same interval is $(1 - r)\Delta t$, then the probability of a population size n at the future time $t + \Delta t$ is

$$p_n(t + \Delta t) = p_{n-1}(t)\,r(n-1)\Delta t + p_n(t)(1 - rn\Delta t) \tag{1.5}$$

Applying the definition of the derivative to Equation 1.5, we then obtain the differential equation

Model III: $$\frac{dp_n}{dt} = r(n-1)p_{n-1} - rnp_n. \tag{1.6}$$

This, in turn, leads to an application of the negative binomial distribution and to the following distribution function:

$$f(n, t) = \binom{n-1}{N_0 - 1} e^{-N_0 r t}(1 - e^{-rt})^{n-N_0}. \qquad (1.7)$$

From Equation 1.7 we can calculate the mean and variance of the population as

$$m(t) = N_0 e^{rt} \qquad (1.8)$$

and

$$\sigma^2(t) = N_0 e^{rt}(e^{rt} - 1). \qquad (1.9)$$

Note that the probabilistic mean (Equation 1.8) is identical to the deterministic solution (Equation 1.2) to Model I. There is no deterministic counterpart to the variance (Equation 1.9) of Model III, however.

Model III approaches the stochastic growth process from the perspective of continuous time. The discrete time version of this stochastic process addresses situations in which the measurements are separated by significant lengths of time (τ), or in which generational occurrences are inherent to the process itself—such as electoral events at regularly timed intervals. Such processes are referenced here as Model IV.

Model IV: probability of 1 event = $r\tau$

probability of 0 event = $1 - r\tau$

$$(1.10)$$

As with continuous stochastic processes, the discrete version of Model IV has a mean that is identical to the value of the deterministic model for discrete time (Model II). Moreover, when the number of events (or population size) is large, the root-mean-square relative fluctuations around the mean are insignificant (May, 1974, p. 33).

Alternatively, stochastic variability can enter a model when the parameters are not fixed longitudinally. Typically, actual parameter values fluctuate randomly around mean values and, in fact, this situation is true of virtually all models. Often it is possible to specify (and thus substitute) a functional form for a parameter that includes a stochastic variable, thereby minimizing the overall degree of stochasticity experienced in the estimation process (see Brown, 1991, pp. 55-56 and 143). It is this refinement that is particularly useful in the highly nonlinear settings discussed here. Operationally, and with respect to Model I, this is expressed as

Model V:
$$\frac{dN}{dt} = r(t)N(t).$$
(1.11)

In practice, however, fixed mean parameter values are usually approximated for specified periods of time. This causes no inherent difficulty so long as the degree of stochasticity within the distributional ranges of the parameters is not large.

The Argument in Favor of the Deterministic Approach

The essential substantive difference between the deterministic approach of Models I and II and that of their stochastic counterparts is that the latter yields probabilities of complete events whereas the former can lead to fractions of events. This difference generally causes no harm in nearly all situations except those with very small event counts or sample sizes. Thus, when populations are even modestly large, the deterministic approach is more than adequate. (See Mesterton-Gibbons, 1989, for a detailed discussion of this difference.)

However, a technical comparison of the deterministic and stochastic models yields additional valuable insights. Recall that the mean value of Model III is identical to the deterministic value for $N(t)$ in Equation 1.2. Also, recall that the variance of the stochastic form (Equation 1.9) is absent from the deterministic version. In general, it is this variance that is lost from the deterministic calculations found in Models I and II, but understand that this is the only thing that is lost.

Because of the availability of a formula for the variance, Models III and IV are modestly superior to their deterministic counterparts in terms of descriptive richness. But the cost of this additional information is gained at considerable expense in calculation, as is evidenced by the computation involved with Equation 1.7. (And this is for a simple model!) Moreover, this added information is of little or no value if our primary concern is the behavioral characteristics of the associated dynamics of change, as compared with, say, our chances of losing our money on a bet in a gambling casino. (See also the final chapter in Coleman, 1964.)

An even bigger issue is at stake than the loss of a formula for a variable's variance. More complicated models quickly become mathematically intractable in the probabilistic setting, forcing researchers to compromise their specifications by using simpler and less substantively satisfying approaches to theory building. Anyone familiar with modeling from a probabilistic perspective will state that the worst error that can be made with any model is a specification error. In the presence of misspecification, no estimate is reliable. Yet it is precisely because of the convenience of linear models (because of their mathematical simplicity and the ease with which probabilistic assumptions may be inserted into them) that researchers often seriously depart from isomorphic parallels between social theory and nonlinear algebraic formalisms, leading them into the most dangerous of terrains.

In many respects, the loss of a formula for a variable's variance is a small price to pay for the nonlinear specification flexibility that is possible using deterministic mathematics. Indeed, it is far better to model a social phenomenon correctly using deterministic algebra, thereby gaining a realistic understanding of the complexity of the underlying social dynamics, than it is to make a linearized mess of the specification while simultaneously maintaining the fantasy of probabilistic completeness because of the algebraic availability of a now worthless measure of variance.

Should there still be resistance to the idea of abandoning the probabilistic approach in the face of significant specification challenges, one should remember that standard statistical methods often have deterministic origins. For example, ordinary least squares (OLS) is based on a deterministic formulation for an equation of a line. Minimizing the sums of squares around this line, operationalized via the normal equations, has no probabilistic basis. Probability is layered into the analysis at a later stage in order to proceed with matters of statistical inference.

The current popularity of maximum likelihood estimation techniques is in large part a response to the lack of theoretically based probabilistic assumptions that are associated with the algebraic structure of OLS linear models. Yet even the most ardent supporters of this approach often recognize the practical limits imposed by the difficulty of working with probabilistic assumptions within settings involving complex algebraic specifications that are substantively motivated, often suggesting instead that researchers borrow more commonly available distributions for which the mathematical properties are known (e.g., King, 1989, p. 56). But with situations of complex social phenomena, this leads us back to the same problem of compromising the substantively derived algebra in order to maintain known mathematical properties of simpler probabilistic models, which ultimately begs the question of why one bothered to understand the social complexity in the first place because the discovery is being so quickly discarded.

Chaos and catastrophe theories directly address the social scientists' need to understand classes of nonlinear complexities that are certain to appear in social phenomena. The probabilistic properties of many chaos and catastrophe models are simply not known, and there is little likelihood that general procedures will be developed soon to alleviate the difficulties inherent with probabilistic approaches in such complicated settings. My own view is that it is better to understand the complexities of human culture using deterministic mathematics than to sacrifice that greater goal for the benefit of the appealing but less useful achievement of probabilistic richness.

With this said, however, one should recognize that the embrace of deterministic mathematics in order to understand human cultural complexity does not mean that we abandon statistical practices altogether. Indeed, deterministic models maintain a complete collection of statistical measures with which the models are evaluated (e.g., measures of fit, tests of the significance of the parameters, measures of relative importance of the parameters). On a practical level, complex nonlinear models require the application of nonlinear least squares procedures, important generic versions of which are described in detail in this volume.

In summary, Models I through V identify a diversity of approaches to modeling longitudinal processes. The highly nonlinear processes described in this volume are addressed primarily using the deterministic approaches of Models I and II but also occasionally V in situations in which parameters are written as functions of other variables containing stochastic components. These approaches permit the algebraic flexibility that is required in these relatively complex nonlinear settings.

2. WHAT IS CHAOS?

In its essence, chaos is an irregular oscillatory process. Because chaos is a subset of the more general classification of oscillatory dynamics, it is useful—before venturing into chaos—to review briefly the extent to which regular oscillatory processes influence human behavior.

Many behaviors that are repeated can be described as some form of a regular oscillatory process. Such processes include our daily cycles of waking and sleeping, going to classes or work, eating our meals, and spending time with our families. Other processes have longer cycles, such as our weekly participation in worship services and our attendance at school at the beginning of each new term. We also vote in cycles. In the United States, citizens vote for Congress every two years and for the president every four. Some people go on diets or begin exercise programs in cycles, both regular and irregular. Indeed, nearly everything we do in life, we do again, be it from the way we look out of our window in the middle of the afternoon to the way we make love. We all have regular periodicity of some sort in our lives, and its routine quality often gives us comfort.

Yet sometimes we do not repeat ourselves even approximately in an orderly repetitive fashion, and thus our behavior occasionally is not regular with regard to time. Insomniacs often consider this a problem with regard to their abilities to obtain sufficient rest each and every night. Extreme irregularity in food consumption can lead to eating disorders. Yet other irregular patterns are more benign, and even pleasant. Irregularity in our thought patterns can lead to our having new insights as we make important new scientific discoveries. Indeed, one characteristic of creativity is the ability of individuals to depart from previously established patterns of thought in order to solve difficult problems with innovative solutions. The daily volatility of our stock markets attracts investors who keep attuned to the longitudinal vagaries of our planet's corporate wealth. And who would doubt that even making love would lose its luster in the absence of all unpredictability? Indeed, both regular and irregular oscillatory patterns dominate most of the dynamics of our lives, and the current interest in chaos among social scientists reflects a growing awareness of this fact of our existence.

Necessary Conditions for Chaos

This chapter introduces chaotic dynamics in two mathematical settings. The first involves a single nonlinear difference equation, and the second involves a nonlinear system of three interdependent differential equations. These two settings are chosen from a heuristic perspective, because all of the primary characteristics of chaos can be demonstrated with these relatively simple models.

In continuous time, the possibility of chaos normally requires a minimum of three independent variables. This means that any continuous time chaotic system will consist of three differential equations. This requirement can be changed in special cases if the system also has a forced oscillator or time lags, in which case chaos can appear even in single equation continuous time models. But the general rule of three equations is the better one to follow for introductory purposes, even though creative applications will certainly employ these other features as well in many modeling situations.

On the other hand, nonlinear difference equations can encounter chaos in one dimension (i.e., one independent variable, and thus one equation). The reason is that difference equations are less stable than their differential equation counterparts because of the lapse of time between consecutive observations.

In addition to dimensionality requirements, chaos can occur only in nonlinear situations. In multidimensional settings, this means that at least one term in one equation must be nonlinear while also involving several of the variables. With all linear models, solutions can be expressed as combinations of regular and linear periodic processes, but nonlinearities in a model allow for instabilities in such periodic solutions within certain value ranges for some of the parameters.

Indeed, this is related to the primary reason for the delay in studying chaos, a point made by Baker and Gollub (1990, p. 3) and relevant to all nonlinear models. Most nonlinear models (and nearly all of the substantively interesting ones) have no analytical solutions. These types of models must be investigated using numerically intensive methods that require computers. It is only recently that computers have become fast enough to allow scientists to examine seriously the complicated dynamic behavior of even simple nonlinear models.

The dimensionality and nonlinearity requirements of chaos do not guarantee its appearance. At best, these conditions allow it to occur, and even then under limited conditions relating to particular parameter values. But this does not imply that chaos is rare in the real world. Indeed, discoveries are being made constantly of either the clearly identifiable or arguably persuasive appearance of chaos. Most of these discoveries are being made with regard to physical systems, but the lack of similar discoveries involving human behavior is almost certainly due to the still developing nature of nonlinear analyses in the social sciences rather than the absence of chaos in the human setting.

Characteristics of Chaos

Chaos has three fundamental characteristics. They are (a) irregular periodicity, (b) sensitivity to initial conditions, and (c) a lack of predictability. These characteristics interact within any one chaotic setting to produce highly complex nonlinear variable trajectories. I demonstrate each of these characteristics below variously using two separate potentially chaotic models, one for discrete time and one for continuous time.

Irregular periodicity refers to the absence of a repeated pattern in the oscillatory movements of the chaotically driven variables. The most direct way to test for this type of periodicity is to examine the periodogram of the Fourier series for the transformed data, a procedure that is outlined in the next chapter. Yet a Fourier analysis does not always work well with chaotic data, and the use of this procedure does not typically lead to "certifiable" results, in the sense of clearly identifying a chaotic process. Rather, the Fourier analysis helps to build a case that a chaotic process has been detected, in the sense that a lawyer would collect evidence regarding a client.

Interestingly, some of the most useful procedures for identifying the complex oscillatory trajectories of potentially chaotic dynamics are also among the easiest to perform. These techniques are graphical in nature, and there are a number of particularly helpful general approaches. The choice of which one to use depends on the dimensionality and type of data.

The nonlinear model that has been among the most well studied with regard to chaos in discrete settings is a general form of a logistic map, and its chaotic properties were initially investigated by May (1976). (The term "map" rather than "function" is used to refer to difference equations because of the discrete way that difference equations associate paired data, i.e., jumping from the value of Y_t to the value of Y_{t+1} without including any values in the continuous range between these points.) This general logistic map is

$$Y_{t+1} = aY_t(1 - Y_t). \tag{2.1}$$

Under the right conditions, this map can produce the standard S-shaped trajectory that is the characteristic feature of all logistic structures. The limit of Equation 2.1 is determined by setting $Y_{t+1} = Y_t = Y^*$, substituting Y^* for all time-subscripted values of Y, and then solving algebraically for Y^*. In general for such a setting, and assuming a relatively low initial condition, the variable Y_t asymptotically approaches the value of its limit from below. If Y_t is above its limit, the subsequent corrective movement is downward.

Oscillations in the trajectory occur when the value of the parameter a is sufficiently large. An example of such a trajectory is given in Figure 2.1. For this figure, the value of the parameter a is 2.8. Note that the trajectory rapidly approaches its limit but then overshoots it. The trajectory then is redirected toward the limit, again passes it, but this time to a lesser extent than before. The oscillations around the equilibrium point continue as the trajectory asymptotically approaches the limit in a convergent fashion.

The oscillatory characteristics of difference equations in one dimension can be analyzed using a graphical procedure called a *stair step diagram*. The stair step diagram that corresponds to Figure 2.1 is presented in Figure 2.2. In this diagram, the vertical axis represents the value of Y_{t+1} whereas the horizontal axis represents Y_t. There are three components to a stair step diagram. The first component is the plot of the first iterates. This is done by computing the values of Y_{t+1} for a continuous range of possible values of Y_t. Because the logistic function is a quadratic from an algebraic perspective, the plot of the first differences naturally produces the form of a parabola. This tell us where the trajectory of the map will go given any previous value.

The second component of a stair step diagram is the 45° line. Because each value of Y_t will become Y_{t+1} in the next iteration, the 45° line represents the place where the values are equal. The use of this line is transparent when the third component of the stair step diagram is introduced into the analysis. To produce the third component, a trajectory is initiated at Y_t on the horizontal axis. The next iterate is computed (i.e., Y_{t+1}) that places the trajectory on the parabola. A horizontal line is then drawn from that point to the 45° line as the value of Y_{t+1} shuffles back to its new algebraic location for Y_t on the horizontal axis in preparation for calculating the next iterate. The next iterate is then calculated, which again places the trajectory on the parabola, followed by a line connecting that point to the 45° line, and so on, until an equilibrium point is effectively reached. Oscillations begin when the horizontal movement to the 45° line places the trajectory above the intersection point of the 45° line and the plot of the first iterates (i.e., the parabola in Figure 2.2). The oscillations in the stair step diagram correspond to oscillations in the longitudinal trajectory as presented in Figure 2.1.

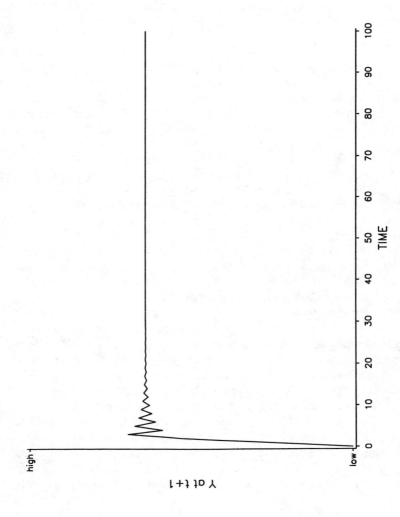

Figure 2.1. The Logistic Difference Equation Time Series Under Nonchaotic Conditions

12

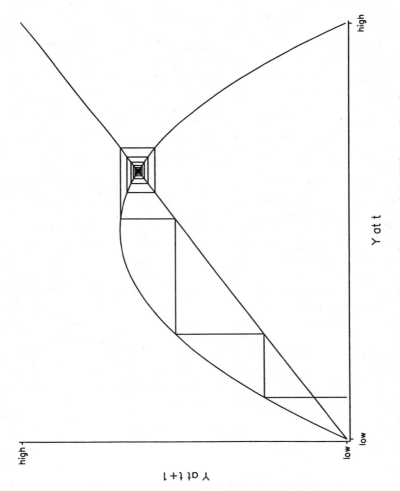

Figure 2.2. The Nonchaotic Stair Step Diagram for the Logistic Difference Equation

13

Stair step diagrams can easily identify regular periodicity among difference equation models. The three basic oscillatory patterns to look for are those that converge to an equilibrium point as in Figures 2.1 and 2.2, those that settle down to repeated finite oscillations that form the shape of one or more squares in the stair step diagram, or chaos. Chaos has its own characteristic signature in these diagrams and is best described via an example.

To demonstrate chaos with the nonlinear difference equation presented above, the value of the parameter a is set equal to 4.0, and the resulting longitudinal trajectory is presented in Figure 2.3. The seemingly random changes in the variable Y_{t+1} over time are central to the nature of discrete time chaotic time series. However, differences between "seemingly random" as compared with "complexly patterned" time series are often difficult to determine visually from the time series alone. The stair step diagram usually resolves this, and the diagram for the current case is presented in Figure 2.4.

In Figure 2.4, the stair step trajectories reveal no clear pattern. However, I stopped the drawing procedure for this diagram after only 100 iterations so that the trajectory would be clearly discernable. Had I let it continue for a larger number of iterations, the entire area outlined in the figure would have been totally covered, indicating that the values of Y_t were covering a continuous range for that variable. This indicates that the oscillations do not settle down into a repeating cycle with a set period, which is, of course, the irregular periodicity aspect of chaotic time series, including those set in continuous time.

The most famous of all continuous time models that can exhibit chaotic behavior is the so-called "Lorenz attractor." This model is a system of three interdependent first order differential equations, and Edward Lorenz originally used it to analyze meteorological phenomena (Lorenz, 1963). There are three state variables (x, y, and z) and three parameters (s, r, and b) in this model. It is presented here as Equations 2.2-2.4.

$$\frac{dx}{dt} = s(y - x) \qquad (2.2)$$

$$\frac{dy}{dt} = rx - y - xz \qquad (2.3)$$

$$\frac{dz}{dt} = xy - bz \qquad (2.4)$$

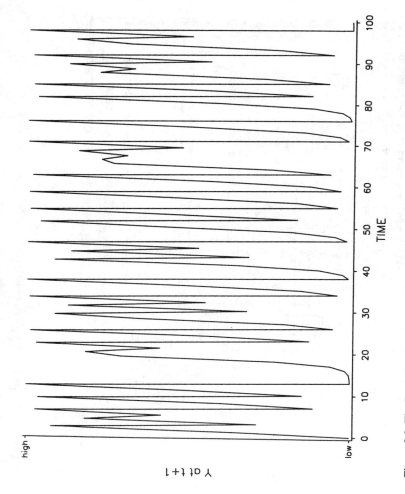

Figure 2.3. The Logistic Difference Equation Time Series Under Chaotic Conditions

15

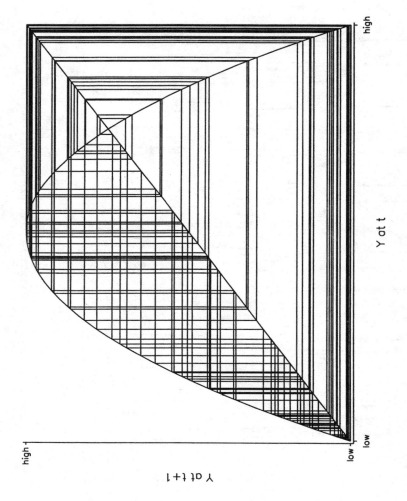

Figure 2.4. The Chaotic Stair Step Diagram for the Logistic Difference Equation

16

Typically, these equations are studied using different values of the parameter r while the parameters s and b are held constant. Here, I follow Lorenz's original practice of using the parameter values $s = 10$ and $b = \frac{8}{3}$. The values of r that are used in numerical investigations fall in the range $0 < r < \infty$. Moreover, with $r < 1$, the origin $(0, 0, 0)$ is globally attracting. When $r > 1$, three zero vectors emerge: the origin (this time an unstable equilibrium point) and two other points. Zero vectors are points in the phase space in which all of the derivatives are equal to zero for the specified combination of the state variables (i.e., x, y, and z). It is with certain values of r above the value 1 that the dynamics of the system become chaotic around the vicinity of these three zero vectors.

These dynamic behaviors can be illustrated using phase diagrams. Phase diagrams are plots in which the state variables are represented on the axes without using a separate axis for time. Thus time is suppressed in phase space representations, and the primary usefulness of these diagrams is to identify patterns in the evolution of the variable values during the continuous flow of the system. Because the above system has three state variables, the phase diagrams for this system typically display three axes.

Figure 2.5 is a phase diagram for the Lorenz system in which the value for parameter r is 16. The initial conditions for the three variables are $x = 0.5$, $y = 0.5$, and $z = 0.5$. Because $r > 1$, the system has three zero vectors. Note that only one of the zero vectors (an attractor) is visible in this figure. A basin is the area in the phase space in which all trajectories move toward an attractor. Thus each attractor has its own basin, or area of attraction. In Figure 2.5, the shown trajectory is caught in the basin of one of the system's two attractors. (Remember that the origin is an unstable equilibrium point, and thus it has no basin.) There is no evidence of chaotic dynamics in this representation of the Lorenz system.

However, if the value of the parameter r is changed to 28, the Lorenz system does display chaotic dynamics. Such a situation is presented in Figure 2.6. It is important to note that increasing the value of the parameter r is the only change from that used to construct Figure 2.5. The trajectory in Figure 2.6 produces a nonrepeating pattern with two primary areas of looping. In the center of each of these looping areas are the attracting zero vectors. Each vector has its own basin, and the trajectory shifts from basin to basin in a seemingly random fashion as it proceeds over time.

Note that there are two tick marks on each of the trajectories in Figures 2.5 and 2.6. Readers should temporarily ignore these marks. They are referenced and explained in Chapter 4 with respect to a discussion on estimating such highly nonlinear models.

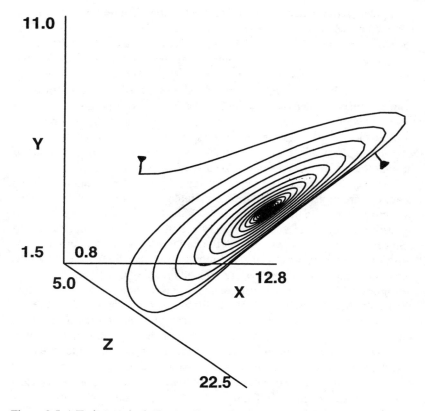

Figure 2.5. A Trajectory in the Lorenz System in Nonchaotic Conditions Is Captured in the Basin of a Single Point Attractor

Because no basin for a single zero vector captures the trajectory, it is necessary to identify this situation with a new term. Because all trajectories in the phase space will be attracted to the combined basins of the two attracting zero vectors, these combined attracting forces constitute what is called a "strange attractor." This type of attractor works similarly to a simple point attractor until the trajectory gets close to it. Once the trajectory arrives in the proximity of a strange attractor, it never settles down into an asymptotic approach to a single point. Rather it continues to orbit all of the attracting zero vectors within the strange attractor in an irregular and nonrepeating fashion.

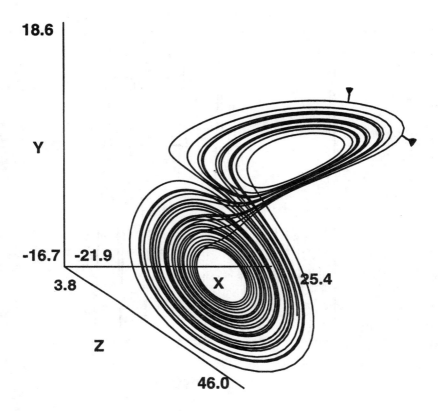

18.6

Y

-16.7 -21.9

3.8

25.4

X

Z

46.0

Figure 2.6. The Classic Lorenz System Strange Attractor

The sensitivity to initial conditions of chaotic systems can be demonstrated using the same parameter combination used to construct Figure 2.6. However, in this case two time series plots are used to show how two different trajectories with very similar initial conditions eventually diverge dramatically.

Figures 2.7 and 2.8 are constructed under identical conditions, except that Figure 2.7 uses the initial conditions $x = 0.5$, $y = 0.5$, and $z = 0.5$, whereas Figure 2.8 changes the initial condition for the variable x to 0.51. Comparing these two figures, note that the first halves of the figures are virtually indistinguishable, in the sense that the trajectories apparently follow the same path. But halfway through, the trajectories suddenly

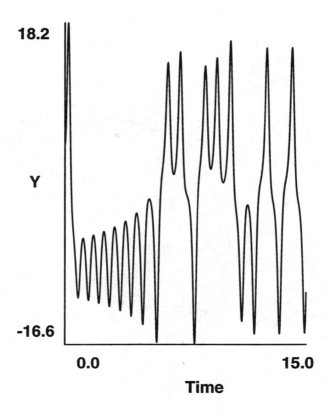

Figure 2.7. A Time Series Plot for Variable y in the Lorenz System in Which the Initial Conditions Are $x = 0.5$, $y = 0.5$, and $z = 0.5$

diverge as their paths take on totally independent directions. This is the nature of chaos. Small changes in the initial conditions in a chaotic system produce dramatically different evolutionary histories.

It is because of this sensitivity to initial conditions that chaotic systems are inherently unpredictable. To predict a future state of a system, one has to be able to rely on numerical calculations and initial measurements of the state variables. Yet slight errors in measurement combined with extremely small computational errors (from roundoff or truncation) make prediction

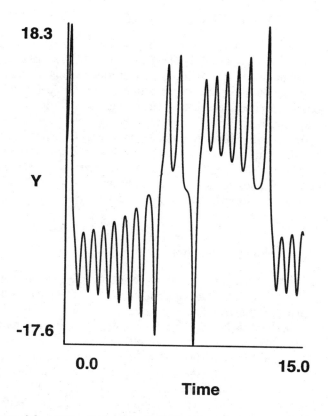

Figure 2.8. A Time Series Plot for Variable y in the Lorenz System in Which the Initial Conditions Are $x = 0.51$, $y = 0.5$, and $z = 0.5$

impossible from a practical perspective. Moreover, small initial errors in prediction grow exponentially in chaotic systems as the trajectories evolve. Thus, theoretically, prediction may be possible with some chaotic processes if one is interested only in the movement between two relatively close points on a trajectory. When longer time intervals are involved, the situation becomes hopeless. This situation has important implications with regard to data requirements for estimating the parameters of chaotic systems, as I discuss more fully in a later chapter.

3. MEASURING CHAOS

There are two basic settings within which chaos can be measured. The first is from the perspective of a set of fully specified equations. The second is with a set of data within which one suspects a chaotic deterministic process may exist. This chapter will describe separate approaches for dealing with chaos from both perspectives. There is no such thing as a definitive set of procedures with regard to analyzing a chaotic time series, because the basic research in this field is still evolving rapidly. Nonetheless, three very useful tools are well established in the relevant literature on chaos, and I describe them all here. These tools are (a) Lyapunov characteristic exponents, (b) Fourier analysis, and (c) the phase space reconstruction of an attractor using data. Additionally, I briefly discuss the spatial correlation test at the end of this chapter.

Lyapunov Characteristic Exponents

Lyapunov characteristic exponents (or, more simply, the Lyapunov exponents) are simple to use and understand, albeit somewhat more difficult to calculate. Basically, the Lyapunov exponents are used to determine quantitatively if chaos exists in a deterministic system. There are as many exponents as there are dimensions, which corresponds with the number of unique variables with time subscripts and the number of equations in the system. It is possible to calculate the Lyapunov exponents both for time series data sets and for nonlinear systems of interdependent equations. I focus here on the application of Lyapunov exponents with fully specified models, because the other methods described in this chapter are being used more regularly with raw data. However, helpful treatments of the use of Lyapunov exponents using data can be found in both McBurnett (in press-a) and Wolf (1986).

For any given nonlinear system, there can exist any number of trajectories in the phase space of that system. (Figure 2.6 presents one example of such a trajectory.) For the purposes of explanation, let us say we have identified a particular trajectory that is associated with a given set of initial conditions and parameter values for a nonlinear system. The Lyapunov exponents tell us whether small changes in the values of the variables for that system produce different trajectories that markedly diverge from the original trajectory. Moreover, in chaotic situations, the Lyapunov exponents tell us that this divergence from the original trajectory is very rapid and, indeed, exponential. This characteristic of chaos is associated with both the sensitivity to initial conditions and the unpredictability aspects of chaos. Thus we get great differences in the histories of our variables because of only minor differences in initial conditions. If one considers any point on the original trajectory as a potential new initial condition from which to begin a new trajectory, it is easy to see that this condition is characteristic of the entire time series and not a result of any unique feature of one particular starting point.

In general, Lyapunov exponents can be positive, negative, or zero. Positive Lyapunov exponents indicate divergence from initial conditions (the chaotic requirement). Negative values for the exponents indicate convergence, and zero indicates neither divergence nor convergence, that is, constancy.

Because there are as many Lyapunov exponents as there are dimensions in the system, the set of exponents for the system is called the spectrum of Lyapunov exponents. Each exponent in the set describes divergence in a separate direction, intuitively (but not technically) comparable to a separate direction along each axis in the phase space.

Strange attractors in three dimensions have the same spectral type: $(+, 0, -)$. This means that there is one positive exponent, one negative exponent, and one zero exponent. Chaos requires at least one positive Lyapunov exponent. In three dimensions, there must be one negative exponent in order to get convergence onto the strange attractor from within its basin of attraction. The zero exponent is required to give topological stability to the attractor. The positive exponent gives divergence *while on* the strange attractor.

In one dimension, the single Lyapunov exponent has the following meanings: positive—chaos, negative—periodic, and zero—marginally stable behavior. In three dimensions, there are the following spectral types: $(+, 0, -)$—chaos, $(0, 0, -)$—a two torus, $(0, -, -)$—a limit cycle, and $(-, -, -)$—a fixed point attractor. In four dimensions, there are three spectral types associated with strange attractors: $(+, +, 0, -)$, $(+, 0, -, -)$, and $(+, 0, 0, -)$.

The approach to calculating the Lyapunov spectrum is not difficult to explain; however, there is more than one approach. The basic idea is the same throughout, even though technical strategies may differ. The current discussion is meant to help readers understand what is going on when the exponents are calculated. However, programmers might desire to supplement these pages with the more technical discussions that can be found in Baker and Gollub (1990), as well as in Wolf (1986) and Wolf, Swift, Swinney, and Vastano (1985).

To establish a heuristically useful setting, let us assume a situation similar to the Lorenz model in which we have three dimensions. Imagine a single trajectory on a strange attractor within the phase space of that system (as with Figure 2.6). Now, consider that each point on that trajectory is a potentially new initial condition, in the sense that we could begin the trajectory from any point on itself and still get the same thing (from that point on, assuming no error in calculation or roundoff). Because this could produce an infinite number of points, let us limit the discussion to those endpoints that are defined by our step size while using the Runge-Kutta for our numerical calculations in preparing the phase diagram. Thus, if we iterate the Runge-Kutta 1000 times using a step size of 0.02 in order to produce a phase diagram, we are calculating 1000 points on the trajectory spanning a time interval of 20 units. (For accuracy purposes, the time span needs to be much longer when actually calculating the Lyapunov exponents.)

Because the Lyapunov exponents summarize the divergence properties throughout the entire trajectory, we need to do our calculations 999 times, and then average the results. We begin by setting up four vectors of three elements each. The first contains our set of initial conditions for our three variables. The remaining three vectors are called an orthonormal frame, which contains the elements (1, 0, 0), (0, 1, 0), and (0, 0, 1). These vectors are an orthonormal frame because they are perpendicular to one another and because they each have a magnitude length of one unit. In its most essential nature, we calculate the Lyapunov exponents from disturbances that are registered in this orthonormal frame as we project into it change among our three original variables. The reason we do not use the raw values of the original variables in the calculation of the Lyapunov exponents is because they become highly correlated over time as they continue to evolve on the strange attractor, thereby distorting any orthogonality properties that may have been assumed among the variables (and that are needed for measurement purposes) when the trajectory was initiated. More accurately, the distance measurement axes needed to evaluate the divergence properties of nearby trajectories become distorted on a strange attractor after a short period of time such that all axes tend to point in the same direction (see Wolf, 1986). Thus we need to measure the variable movements with respect to this orthonormal frame.

One then initiates the Runge-Kutta algorithm to compute the variable trajectories. After each step along the way, it is necessary first to renormalize the first vector (containing the original data values) and then to project the normalized movement along each axis onto the orthonormal frame.

This requires use of the Gram-Schmidt reorthogonalization process (with normalization). The idea is to project the vector for the independent variables onto the orthonormal frame at each stopping point as determined by the step size of the Runge-Kutta. This new orthogonalized vector is then normalized, the log of this norm is taken, and this process is repeated throughout the trajectory while summing all of the logs of the vector norms. Because the procedure projects the original data onto three distinct orthogonal vectors, one ends up with three numbers (i.e., the Lyapunov spectrum) for a three-dimensional system. These Lyapunov exponents for the system then tell us the magnitude of divergence or convergence along each of the orthogonal dimensions as one travels along the trajectory. Computer code using the Basic language for computing Lyapunov exponents is available in the appendix of Baker and Gollub (1990), and in Wolf et al. (1985) using FORTRAN.

Once one has identified the Lyapunov spectrum as chaotic, the question then becomes one of estimating the magnitude of the largest positive Lyapunov exponent to determine the severity of the local divergence properties on the attractor. These magnitudes can be quite varied, given modest changes in the parameter values of the system. To show how varied these magnitudes can be, I calculated the full Lyapunov spectrum for the nonlinear forced pendulum model that is described thoroughly by Baker and Gollub (1990) in their introductory text on chaos. I used a continuous range of values for two of the primary parameters in the model, then plotted the largest Lyapunov exponent on a graph, using a shade to indicate its magnitude. The graph is shaded using shareware imaging software that is available from the National Center for Supercomputing Applications at the University of Illinois at Urbana-Champaign. This graph is presented here as Figure 3.1.

In Figure 3.1, bright shades indicate parametric regions that produce chaotic trajectories in the phase space of this three-dimensional system. From this figure, it is clear that small changes in the values of the parameters can fundamentally alter the dynamic characteristics of the system.

On a practical note, such graphs are not easy to produce. Programming aside, the number of computations necessary to produce such a picture are formidable. The data for Figure 3.1 took two weeks to calculate, using a program written by myself using the Think Pascal compiler and running 24 hours a day on a Macintosh 900. But some pictures are worth almost any effort given their informational content, and chaos tends to be an area of nonlinear mathematics for which this is often the case.

26

high

Parameter
One

low

low   high

Parameter   Two

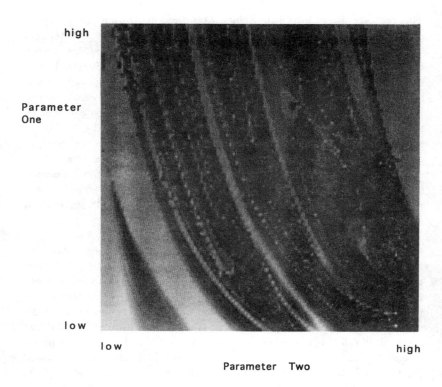

Figure 3.1. Largest Lyapunov Exponents for the Chaotic Pendulum. Bright Shades
Indicate Chaos

Fourier Analysis

Frequency analysis is now an important aspect of social scientific research. In the physical and life sciences, the analysis of frequencies that may be embedded in a body of data has been standard practice for many years. For example, physicists are interested in sound and radiation frequencies, biologists are interested in cycles inherent in, say, predator and prey relationships, and so on. But recent studies by social scientists (e.g., Berry, 1991; Stimson, 1991) indicate that human behavior, both aggregate and individual, often evolves with cyclical characteristics, and to study these characteristics requires an analysis of the associated frequencies. The complex frequency structure of chaotic data can often be discerned using Fourier analysis. Moreover, Fourier analysis can be used either with raw data or with a time series calculated from a fully specified nonlinear system.

There are two relevant definitions for a frequency. Throughout this discussion, I will limit my comments to cyclical changes in variable values with respect to time. A frequency can be the number of instances that an event occurs within some given time period or it can be the number of instances that a periodic function repeats itself in every unit of time. Frequency is the reciprocal of period, and a period is the smallest interval of time after which a periodic function has the same values. Thus frequency = 1/period. For example, for a constant k, $f(t) = f(t + k)$ for all t has a period of k. Thus, if we allow time to be measured in radians (via the wrapping function), then $\sin(t) = \sin(t + 2\pi n)$, where $2\pi n$ is a period of $\sin(t)$ for all integers n. Its principal or smallest period is 2π.

Continuing with the more general example of $f(t) = \sin(\alpha t)$, for $0 \leq t \leq 2\pi$, the period for this function is 2π, with a frequency of $1/(2\pi)$, if we assume (for the moment) that $\alpha = 1$. But let us say that we measure time in terms of 1024 (this number will make sense later) observations, in the sense that we make these equally spaced observations over a span of time. We can then use these observations as our unit of analysis, such that frequency equals either $1/1024$ or $1/(2\pi)$, depending on how we measure time. Measuring time in terms of 1024 units will simply require us to change the value of α in order to complete one period of the *sine* after the appropriate interval. If we wanted a frequency of two times this, we would simply write, frequency = $(1/1024)2 = 1/512$, or one cycle per 512 observation periods. Such small numbers are typical of the slow oscillations (i.e., long waves) found in much social scientific data. Thus a method of estimating frequency over a set period of time with many equally spaced observations is

$$\text{frequency per observation period} = \frac{\text{total \# of cycles}}{\text{total \# of observations}}.$$

Particularly lucid discussions of the technicalities of Fourier analysis can be found in Kaplan (1952) and Kaplan and Lewis (1970). Another clear and useful treatment can be found in McBurnett (in press-b). In general, Fourier methods are used to transform a time series set of data into an algebraic form of the type

$$f(t) = a_0 + \sum_{n=1}^{\infty} [a_n \cos(\omega nt) + b_n \sin(\omega nt)] \qquad (3.1)$$

where $\omega = 2\pi/T$ = the number of cycles in a length of time equal to 2π, and T is the period of the function. ω is often referred to as the *fundamental angular frequency*. The frequency per observation period is ω/(total # of observations). Note also that with time series data, $1 \leq n \leq N$, where N is the total number of observations.

The coefficients a_n and b_n in Equation 3.1 are constants that represent the amplitudes of the various harmonics (i.e., the sinusoidal components in the equation) that have different frequencies. The goal of Fourier analysis is to identify the frequencies and amplitudes of all of the various harmonics. Typically, this type of analysis ends with the construction of a periodogram (discussed later) that is based on these frequencies and amplitudes.

Fourier analysis of most data usually identifies a variety of interacting frequencies (always together with their associated amplitudes) because most phenomena vibrate in correspondence to more than one wave form at the same time. Complex vibrational patterns can produce a tangled mess of interacting harmonics, and it is the task of Fourier analysis to untangle the mess. Completely random oscillations are the most complex of all, and Fourier analysis identifies a long and continuous range of frequencies in such situations.

Figures 3.2 and 3.3 are presented here to illustrate the Fourier analysis of a simple wave form. Figure 3.2 contains the wave form of the sine function. The Fourier analysis of that wave is shown in Figure 3.3. To compute the sine trajectory, I made 1024 observations of the function while it made ten complete cycles from zero to 2π. The number 1024 is used to simplify the calculations involved in the most commonly used implementation of Fourier analysis, the Fast Fourier Transform. This implementation runs most smoothly when the number of observations is a power of 2.

In social scientific work, we often measure time in terms of when the observations of a phenomenon occur, such as when the census is taken or when an election occurs. Thus, if we want to measure time in terms of the 1024 observations, we compute the frequency per observation period as detailed above. In the current setting, this results in 10/1024, or 0.009765 (or approximately 0.01). Note that this is the value on the horizontal axis of Figure 3.3 over which there is a peak in the graph. Figure 3.3 is called the periodogram of the sine function shown in Figure 3.2. It identifies the

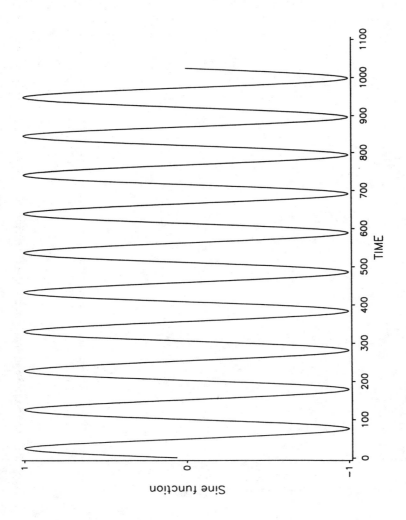

Figure 3.2. The Sine Function

29

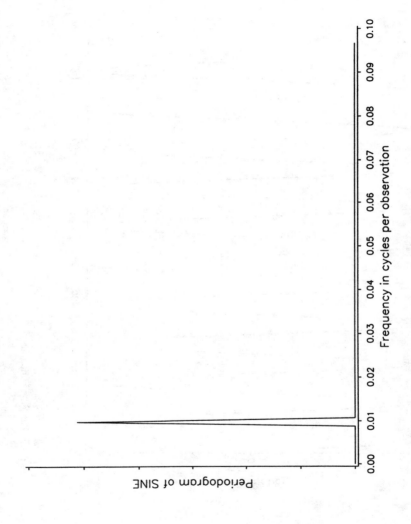

Figure 3.3. The Fourier Periodogram of the Sine Function

frequency and indicates its amplitude via the height of the peak. If the function was more complicated, such as the two frequency function $f(t) = \sin(t) + \sin(0.5t)$, then additional peaks would have appeared in the periodogram (in the latter case, two peaks).

When dealing with random variations in a variable, no clear cyclical patterns should emerge in the periodogram. Figure 3.4 presents a plot of random numbers, and Figure 3.5 is the periodogram of those data. Note that the periodogram identifies no clear frequency pattern; that is, peaks and dips appear as randomly distributed as the original numbers.

The periodogram of chaos can sometimes closely resemble that of random numbers. This is particularly true of maps, such as the nonlinear logistic difference equation. However, the situation is not always so simple, especially with continuous time models. Figures 3.6 through 3.8 contain the periodograms for the three variables in the Lorenz model as depicted in Figure 2.6. Note that the periodograms identify discrete ranges of frequencies within which there seem to be a high concentration of frequencies represented. Thus Fourier analysis is not a clear indicator of chaos, in the sense that the analysis does not always reveal a pattern closely resembling true randomness. It sometimes succeeds in suggesting chaotic conditions by failing to identify any clear pattern of dominant frequencies, but other times it seems to identify a pattern when one may not exist. The astute user of Fourier analysis will look not for a set pattern as a definitive demonstration in this regard but rather for some indication of the presence of complex nonlinearity.

This does not diminish the usefulness of Fourier analysis in analyzing potentially chaotic situations. The case for chaos is rarely cut and dry. Rather, evidence needs to be accumulated for making a case for chaos in a given setting, and Fourier analysis often yields useful insight.

Moreover, under chaotic situations—especially those involving continuous time—identifying a continuous range of frequencies that seem to be highly represented in a body of data is very revealing. Particularly if the range is significantly wide (as is the case with the Lorenz chaotic attractor), this indicates that the associated nonlinear dynamics are quite complex, which, at base, is the essential heart of our interest in chaos. Readers might note with interest one of my own applications of Fourier analysis in which a primary useful ingredient is the standard deviation of the periodogram frequencies as an indicator of nonlinear complexity given a continuous range of certain parameter values in a nonlinear model involving politics and the environment (Brown, 1995, Chapter 6).

text continued on p. 37

32

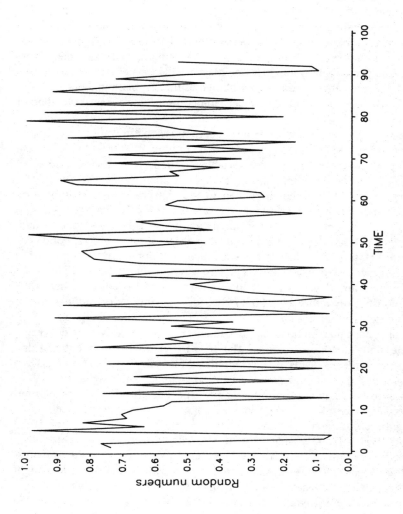

Figure 3.4. A Time Series of Random Numbers

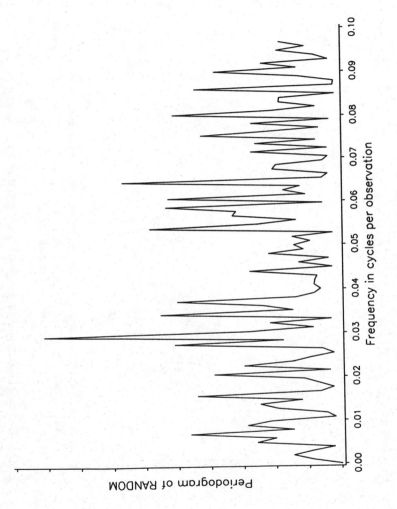

Figure 3.5. The Fourier Periodogram of a Series of Random Numbers

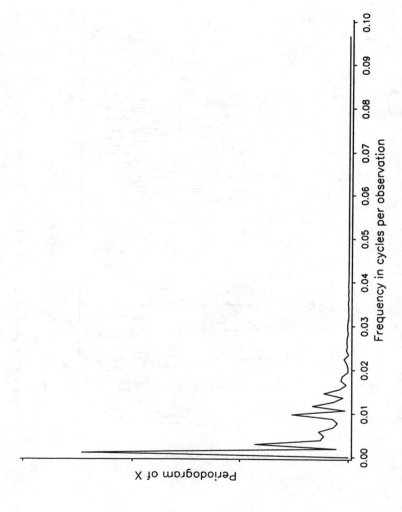

Figure 3.6. The Fourier Periodogram of the Variable x for the Lorenz Chaotic System

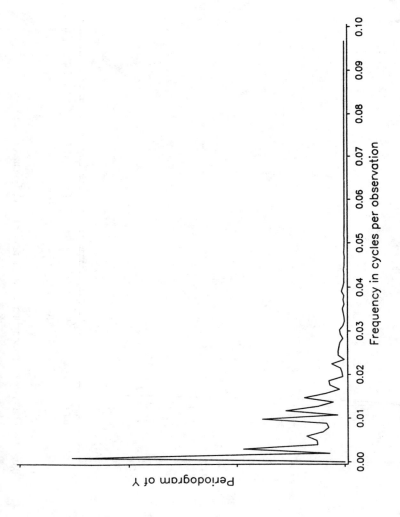

Figure 3.7. The Fourier Periodogram of the Variable *y* for the Lorenz Chaotic System

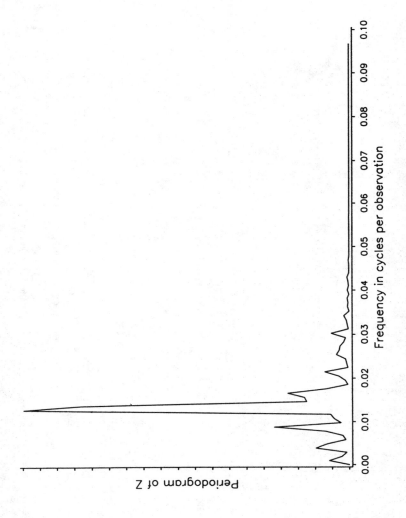

Figure 3.8. The Fourier Periodogram of the Variable z for the Lorenz Chaotic System

Phase Space Reconstruction
of an Attractor Using Data

A simple graphical procedure can be used to identify the existence of a chaotic attractor (or even a periodic oscillator) in a body of data. The procedure can be used on data that result from simulations of a known dynamical system in either discrete or continuous time, but experimental, aggregate, or survey data can work as well. The procedure requires the use of only one variable at a time, and it does not require the a priori knowledge of the formal equations that underlie the dynamics. This procedure acts to reconstruct the shape of a chaotic attractor for visual inspection, even in the presence of substantial amounts of stochastic noise.

To execute the procedure one simply plots the value of a variable on its lag. The length of the lag needs to be determined experimentally. In essence, the researcher is rotating the attractor in its own phase space when picking different values of the lag. With discrete time data, the minimal lag is obviously 1. However, when dealing with very closely spaced measurements that approximate a continuous process (such as a sample of points from a continuous time nonlinear model that is simulated using a Runge-Kutta), the lag can be as small as the step size of the originating algorithm.

This procedure is demonstrated here using the Lorenz continuous time model. The analysis is conducted on the data that are portrayed in Figure 2.6. The analysis will work with any of the three variables but, for brevity, I demonstrate the procedure using the variable x. I use a step size for the Runge-Kutta of 0.01. Although most lags will yield some useful portrait of the attractor, I use a lag of 10 iterations for this illustration.

The phase space reconstruction of the Lorenz chaotic attractor using the variable x is presented in Figure 3.9. To demonstrate how the presence of substantial amounts of white noise does not usually nullify this procedure, I add random variations to this variable and then repeat the plotting procedure. The results of this are presented in Figure 3.10.

Note that in both Figures 3.9 and 3.10 the Lorenz attractor is clearly apparent. Substantially greater amounts of noise (up to some limit, of course) still yield a recognizable attractor shape. Indeed, interested readers should note that McBurnett (in press-a, in press-b) has used this procedure with considerable success using public opinion survey data relating to the 1984 presidential primary elections in the United States. More technical treatments of the procedure can be found in Packard, Crutchfield, Farmer, and Shaw (1980) and Takens (1981).

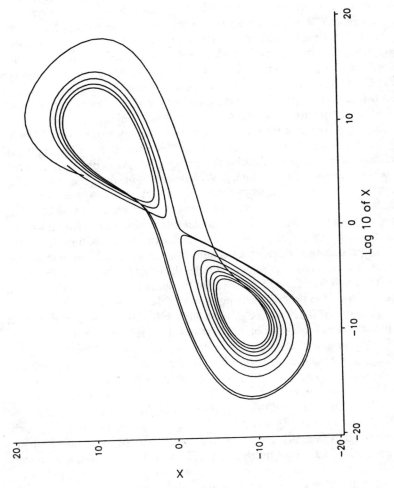

X

Lag 10 of X

Figure 3.9. The Phase Space Reconstruction of the Lorenz Attractor Using *x* and Its Lag

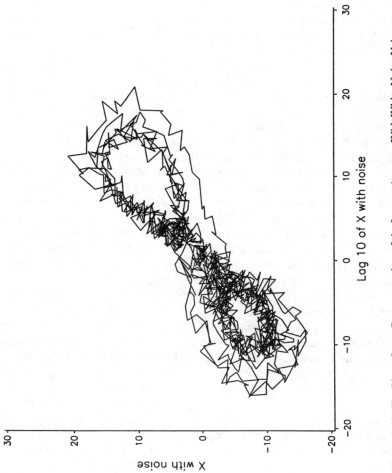

Figure 3.10. The Phase Space Reconstruction of the Lorenz Attractor With White Noise Using x and Its Lag

The Spatial Correlation Test

There is another technique that is increasingly being discussed in the social scientific literature that is designed to discover chaotic attractors that may be embedded within a time series. In this sense, its use is similar to that of the graphical technique explained above. This technique involves the calculation of a specific statistic that is used to conduct the spatial correlation test.

With the spatial correlation test, one can discover the location of a chaotic attractor in a body of time series data. But, as with the above graphical method, the researcher is still left with the problem of specifying the equations that can reproduce this attractor analytically. Nonetheless, both the phase space reconstruction of a chaotic attractor and the spatial correlation test are useful in helping to identify the scope of the substantive problem. If a researcher determines that a chaotic attractor has been identified using a variety of techniques, then the accumulation of evidence using these techniques supports the idea of pursuing further investigations.

The spatial correlation test, also occasionally referenced as the ball counting technique, determines the relationship between each point in a time series and all of the other points in the series. The goal is to determine the dimension of the attractor. This information is important because, once it is obtained, the researcher knows how many independent variables (and, thus, equations) are necessary to model the dynamical process.

In chaotic processes, the dimension of the attractor is not an integer. For example, the spatial correlation test may indicate that the dimension of an attractor is, say, 2.54. A statistical test needs to be used in the procedure to ensure that this number is, in fact, statistically different from an integer at a reasonable confidence level. Then, to know how many independent variables are involved in this problem, we use the next highest integer over the system's calculated dimension. Thus, in the current example, three independent variables, and thus three equations, are needed to model the relevant dynamics. In this way, this data analytic procedure can assist the modeling enterprise by offering a minimal level of guidance with regard to the number of variables that need to be included in a model of the entire process.

Readers who desire a more technical discussion of the spatial correlation test, together with programming tips, should consult Richards (1992) as well as McBurnett (in press-a).

4. ESTIMATING CHAOS MODELS

This chapter describes an approach to estimating nonlinear interdependent systems with chaotic potential using nonlinear least squares. The situation is one in which a data set with many temporal measures exists for a set of variables. Although this chapter uses the Lorenz system as an example, the procedures are quite general and can be used in any number of nonlinear settings. I return to a related application of these methods of estimation in a later chapter with respect to catastrophe models. Indeed, nonlinear least squares procedures can also work for linear models. However, because one of the primary reasons for using linear models in the first place is to avoid the computational difficulty of these techniques, it makes no sense to use nonlinear least squares with anything except nonlinear models.

Nonlinear least squares is actually a subset of a larger collection of optimization methods that is usually described as *numerical methods for unconstrained optimization*. A number of superb introductory treatments of these techniques are available, although none have been marketed in the direction of the social scientific community. Two books by Hamming (1971, 1973) are particularly noteworthy, as is an edited volume by Murray (1972). (See also Brown, 1991, Appendix; 1995, Appendix.)

In general, nearly all numerical methods for optimizing some function begin with an initial set of parameter estimates. Some procedure is then used to produce a series of new estimates in which each sequential estimate is better than the previous one. The differences in methods usually revolve around the procedure that is used to produce the new series of improving estimates. The most common procedure is to base the new estimates on the first partial derivatives of the function relative to changes in the parameter values, and it is this procedure that is described here.

Thus, to proceed, a function is required for optimization. This function is not the model itself but the fit of the model to the data. Because the fit of the model can be determined only if there are estimates for the parameters (which we do not yet have), we need some initiating procedure to produce something with which we can begin. The standard practice is to use a random number generator to guess values for each of the parameters in the model from within plausible ranges. The sequence of improved estimates mentioned above is thus initiated from these guessed starting points. Because of nonlinearities in the fit surface itself, it is necessary to initiate the entire estimation procedure many times with new initial guesses in order to ensure that the global maximum to the fit surface has been located. I return to this latter point later.

Using the guessed initial conditions for the parameter values, the model is projected forward in time to produce a time series for each of the variables. For a continuous time situation, this is done using a numerical technique such as a fourth order Runge-Kutta. Given the fact that the initial parameter values were simply guesses, the predicted values of these variables are not likely to be anywhere near those of the actual data, and one should not be disappointed with an abysmal initial model fit. The optimization function itself is calculated as

$$\text{FIT} = 1 - \frac{\text{RSS}}{\text{TSS}} \tag{4.1}$$

Here, FIT represents the fit of the model to the data, RSS is the residual sums of squares with respect to the model and data, and TSS is the total sums of squares as computed from the data alone. This function is comparable to the R^2 statistic for linear models. However, with linear models, RSS can never be greater than TSS, because TSS is based on deviations from the variable mean, and no relationship between a model and the data produces a linear slope of zero that retrieves the mean as the best predictor for the dependent variable. With nonlinear least squares, RSS can be very large because of the initial (and undoubtedly incorrect) guesses for the parameter values. Intuitively, one has sent the model in a direction very far from the data, and the residuals can be quite large. Thus the value for FIT can be negative in the beginning of these types of procedures, which is why the label R^2 is not used in the nonlinear setting.

In the situation of the Lorenz model, there are three variables. Thus there will be three values for FIT, one for each variable. In practice, these values will not be numerically close, at least not at first. Partial derivatives for FIT are then calculated numerically with respect to each of the parameters in the model. This is done for each parameter, one at a time. First, the value for one of the parameters is reduced by some small amount below its initially guessed value. (Often 0.0001 is used, but there is no hard and fast rule here. The actual amount of the disturbance that is useful in a given situation depends on the scales used.) Then the value of FIT is calculated. Next, the value of the same parameter is increased by the same amount over its initially guessed value, and the value of FIT is again computed. For that single parameter, one now has two values for FIT as well as two values for the parameter that were used in calculating these values for FIT. The difference between the two values for FIT as well as the difference between the two values of the given parameter are then calculated via simple subtraction. The partial derivative of the fitting function with respect to the parameter in question is then evaluated as the change in the model's fit divided by the change in the parameter.

The procedure for calculating the partial derivative of the fitting function with respect to the parameter is repeated for each of the parameters separately (i.e., one at a time). One then has a collection of partial derivatives, one for each parameter. These are typically arranged as a vector and used to produce the series of improved estimates for the parameters. This is accomplished using a first order Runge-Kutta technique, commonly referenced as the Euler method. The actual relation between one estimate and the next in the sequence is

$$\text{BNEXT} = B + j(\text{PARTIALS}), \qquad (4.2)$$

in which B is the collection of initial parameter values arranged as a vector, **BNEXT** is the vector containing the next in the sequence of parameter value improvements, **PARTIALS** is the vector of partial derivatives of the fitting function that is to be optimized, and j is a small number that is used to make gradual changes in the parameter values. The value of j is somewhat arbitrary, but it is usually customary to have it vary so that it is relatively small when the partials are particularly large (as in the beginning of the estimation procedure when guessed values for the parameters are used). Again, although there is no hard and fast rule, typical values for j tend to vary between 0.1 and 0.000001, with 0.001 being a common starting point for many social scientific situations.

Following the recipe of Equation 4.2, the values of the parameters are modified until improvements no longer occur. At that point, the partials of the fitting function are taken again and the march continues with a new collection of partial derivatives giving the required directional guidance. This can go on almost indefinitely, of course, because one approaches the optimum of the fitting function asymptotically.

Thus it is necessary to come up with a means of stopping the overall procedure. Often scientists and engineers set some a priori criterion with regard to the partials, such as when the sums of squares of the partials go below some given number. But, again, hard and fast rules do not exist, and often the best procedure may be simply to let the estimation routine run through a sufficiently long series of iterations in which one keeps track of the number of times that the computer program computes the partial derivatives of the fitting function. The more the better, and accuracy constraints usually evaporate when one has free access to a fast mainframe computer. To offer a rough rule of thumb, I have found that 50 returns to the section of the program that calculates the partials of the fitting function often yields sufficient accuracy to allow one to proceed with the analysis of a system's dynamics. There have been occasions in which I raised that number to 200 and beyond, however.

When economy is a primary concern, the first approach of setting a criterion for the partials may be worth the effort. Nonetheless, one should be forewarned that this approach often fails in situations in which the choice for the value of j in Equation 4.2 is set unnecessarily too small, and computer time is consumed inefficiently. In any case, it is always good advice to write one's computer code such that the procedure can be monitored along the way and adjustments can be made using new runs without waiting for poorly performing runs to finish.

At this point, one can say that a maximum of the fitting function has been obtained using a final set of parameter values (i.e., the last in the improved series). However, nonlinearities in the fitting hypersurface are often such that no guarantee exists that any one run of the estimation program (using one set of initial starting points for the parameter values) leads to the global maximum of the fitting function. Thus one may have arrived at only a local maximum of the function. The practice of repeating the entire estimation procedure many times using a different set of initial parameter guesses each time is the standard safeguard to use in most situations. Following this procedure, one simply saves the results of the estimation run that yields the highest final value for FIT, discarding the results of all other runs. It is also common for researchers to discard runs that yield theoretically implausible (or impossible) estimated parameter values (see Przeworski & Sprague, 1986, Appendix).

Again, there is no hard and fast rule as to how many runs one should attempt in order to be reasonably certain that the global maximum of the fitting function has been located. In general, however, one can stop estimating the model when the estimation procedure tends to return close approximations to the highest achieved value for FIT with final parameter values being similar. Actual practice can be quite varied, however. Sprague conducted literally thousands of runs before stopping the estimation procedure used for *Paper Stones* (Przeworski & Sprague, 1986, p. 188). Given the fact that this effort was a first of its kind in the social sciences, it is understandable that the authors wanted to err on the side of safety. On the other hand, I have found that a few hundred runs will usually do for most nonlinear problems typical to the social sciences. Again, much depends on the particular problem at hand.

The Problem of Step Size

A remaining problem is how to structure the relationship between the data and the model with respect to time. In the continuous time setting, a Runge-Kutta will most likely be used to extend the model through time, thereby producing a time series of predicted points for the variables. But the actual data are measured observations taken, we hope (for the sake of computational ease), at equally spaced intervals. The problem is that if one makes the step size for the Runge-Kutta too large, the estimates for the parameter values will have to shrink proportionally in order to restrain the speed of the variable trajectories, thereby leading to incorrect estimates. On the other hand, making the step size too small leads to computational inefficiencies.

My own bias is to err on the side of wasting computer time whenever there is any doubt regarding the best step size. A useful rule of thumb is to use a small step size and allow the Runge-Kutta to proceed for a complete time unit between each observation in the data set. For example, if the step size is 0.1, ten iterations of the Runge-Kutta between each observation will lead to the completion of 1 time unit (10×0.1) between observations. However, chaotic attractors often require much smaller step sizes to allow for numerical accuracy along the highly nonlinear trajectories. Thus if a step size of 0.01 is used, the Runge-Kutta could be allowed to proceed through 100 iterations before the model's predicted values for the variables are compared with the actual data. But again, experimentation is required before making a final decision as to the best values to use for a given problem. Sometimes it may be desirable to use a small step size and to extend the trajectory through only a few iterations before comparing the model's predicted values with the data.

Comparing the Model's Predicted Values to the Data

At the end of each time unit (e.g., after 100 iterations of the Runge-Kutta using a step size of 0.01), the model's predicted values need to be compared with the next in the sequence of actual data values. The FIT for the model is computed across all of these comparisons throughout the entire time series, and it is at this point that real trouble may occur.

The very nature of chaotic time series makes them highly susceptible to measurement problems. I am not referring here to the problem of making accurate measurements when collecting the original data, although this is a serious and related matter. The real problem affecting social scientific analyses relates to the unpredictability of chaotic dynamics given a sufficiently long time interval between one point in the series and the next. Chaotic time series are sometimes very predictable if one stays close enough to a previously measured point, a phenomenon often referenced as local predictability. The trouble occurs when extrapolating too far from that point. *If the time series measurements are not made sufficiently close together, it may be impossible to estimate even a correctly specified model because it may not be possible to generate an accurate predicted time series from the model.* Even small inaccuracies in the parameter estimates can send the predicted time series "off the deep end," so to speak.

This is an important point to make in this setting because it directly concerns the way social scientists collect their data. Social scientific data tend to be measured after long intervals of time. One of the reasons for this is cost. Grant money is usually needed to conduct large-scale social surveys, and such money is typically not available for projects requiring long periods of time with many waves of observations and many cases. For example, the 1980 National Election Panel Study for the U.S. electorate had four waves of interviews combined with a substantial number of cases, but this type of study has never been repeated (largely for financial reasons), and four waves is hardly adequate to investigate chaotic dynamics. Aggregate data may not be much better because such measures are usually taken after long periods of time (e.g., every ten years for most censuses, and every few years for elections).

Thus social scientists have a particularly severe problem with regard to data. A scientist in the physical sciences can usually recalibrate some instrument to make observations at more closely defined intervals, but social scientists have no machinery to recalibrate. We are limited by the data that exist, and we may need to change the way we collect our data if we wish to estimate nonlinear dynamical systems with truly chaotic potential.

Because the above point is so important to how we proceed with so many of our current data related activities, I conducted my own numerical experiments using the Lorenz model to determine how far apart the observations of the data could be before nonlinear least squares could no longer easily estimate the parameters. To create the data for this experiment, I set the step size for a fourth order Runge-Kutta at 0.02 and projected the model through 1024 iterations while using Lorenz's original set of parameter values. I then sampled every nth observation to create a data set of a truly chaotic time series measured at various intervals.

The results of my experiment indicate that nonlinear least squares has no difficulty in accurately estimating the model's parameter values for samples of up to every 7th observation in the series. However, when sampling every 8th observation, the procedure quickly becomes lost in the nonlinear complexities of the problem and I was not able to recover the original parameter values, despite my trying a number of initial parameter assignments (including some very close to the actual real parameter values). Moreover, it is important to remember that I used the same model in the estimation program that was used to generate the data. Thus the problem is not of the model specification variety. Rather, the problem is inherent to the phenomenon of chaos itself.

This problem of estimating chaos is related to the size of the largest positive Lyapunov exponent. This exponent will change from one model to the next, and it will vary markedly for the same model using different parameter values. Because the exponent captures how fast system memory is lost, systems with higher values of this exponent will be both highly nonlinear and very difficult to predict. The estimation program needs to predict a future point on a trajectory from a current point. The larger the value of the Lyapunov exponent, the closer these two points need to be in order for the estimation procedure to be successful.

To demonstrate this relationship between the degree of a system's nonlinearity and the ability to estimate the parameters for the system given variously spaced measurements of the variables, refer again to Figures 2.5 and Figures 2.6. The two tick marks on each of the trajectories on these figures indicate the maximum allowable distances between the measurements of the variables given the parameter values that are used to compute each trajectory. Both figures are constructed using the Lorenz system, but the parameter values used for Figure 2.5 do not produce chaos whereas the parameter values used for Figure 2.6 do produce chaos. Note that the distance between the two tick marks in Figure 2.5 is much longer than that between the tick marks in the chaotic situation presented in Figure 2.6. In Figure 2.6, it becomes impossible to estimate the parameter values after the distance between each measurement of the variables exceeds seven iterations of the Runge-Kutta, or 0.14 units of time. The situation does not become unmanagable under the nonchaotic conditions of Figure 2.5 until the distance between the variable measurements exceeds 20 Runge-Kutta iterations, or 0.4 units of time. The rule of thumb here is that closer measurements are always better, with matters becoming absolutely critical in highly nonlinear situations.

The Future of Chaotic Studies in the Social Sciences

It is not clear how chaos will be applied in social scientific analyses. Personally, I am intuitively certain that chaotic social phenomenon do occur, probably more regularly than we might suspect. But because of its very nature, and because social scientists have limited access to the resources needed to collect the type of data that may be required to estimate such models fully, we may only rarely certifiably identify fully specified formal systems with chaotic behavioral characteristics. But there is one type of situation that may be open to us that frees us from these unhappy constraints.

Fortunately, from the perspective of those who want to find evidence of chaos in social settings, many social phenomena evolve slowly, with periodic characteristics approaching decades, or even centuries and beyond. In situations in which the social phenomena have long and chaotic periodic properties, it may be that our own normal measurements of social indicators—both individual and aggregate—will be sufficiently closely spaced to allow for an adequate setting for parameter estimation. In such cases, census information may be more than adequate, for example. With this realization comes another problem, however. We may have to wait a long time for such data to be available, because long periodic properties require measurements of the long-term evolution of our societies. But some variable histories may already be satisfactory for such purposes, and more than a few of us look hopefully toward a future in which both the lucky and the brilliant make these important empirical discoveries.

Nonetheless, even in the absence of adequately measured data, chaos has an important role to play in future social scientific research. Formal models of social systems displaying chaotic properties can be fully investigated now from an analytic point of view using simulations. Indeed, among my own analyses, I investigate the possibility that potentially disastrous nonlinear dynamics (both chaotic and nonchaotic) dominate the relationship between democratic electoral politics and the environment (Brown, 1994; 1995). In such a situation we do not want to wait until a complete collection of data are available to us, because the outcome may be one of species suicide. Rather, the model helps us understand our current situation so as to allow us to change our evolutionary course and capture a better future for ourselves and our environment.

Moreover, situations may arise in which chaotic attractors may be empirically located in sets of data (using some of the techniques discussed in the previous chapter) long before we have an adequate formal specification of the processes that caused them. Such a case has been made by McBurnett (in press-a, in press-b) using data from the 1984 NES Continuous Monitoring U.S. presidential study, and I can only assume that similar situations will arise repeatedly in the future.

Thus for nonlinear social science to progress in the area of chaos requires some degree of faith, at least in the short term. In my view, social scientists need to be open to the possibility that human behavior—both long term and short term—may be as nonlinear as are the dynamic properties of the remainder of the manifest universe. Moreover, it is necessary to believe that this possibility is sufficiently high to warrant an extended period of scientific investigation regarding such dynamics, recognizing that any such discoveries along these lines will be hard won and perhaps rare. Faith in the possibility has to be strong enough to engender the level of patience that may be required to make these exceedingly important breakthroughs in our understanding of our own existence.

An Alternative Approach for Maps

Nonlinear least squares can be used for maps as well as continuous time models. However, in some circumstances it may be possible for researchers to use simpler methods to estimate the parameters of maps. Whereas some researchers have suggested the use of somewhat complicated procedures (such as singular-value decomposition) for use with potentially chaotic data (e.g., see Crutchfield & McNamara, 1987; Mees, 1992), McBurnett (1994) has conducted a large number of experiments (literally thousands) using both OLS and its cousin, SUR (seemingly unrelated regression), for map data, both with and without the inclusion of stochastic noise. Using both the logistic map and the two-dimensional Henon map, he has demonstrated that these relatively simple procedures can successfully estimate known parameter values with great precision. However, it is interesting to note that the precision of the estimates varies directly with the degree of stochastic noise that is added to the variables.

Given these promising results, it is probably worth the effort for researchers to investigate using OLS or SUR in situations using data with long time series. Nonlinear least squares can always be attempted as an alternative approach, but given the possibility of this approach encountering a potentially intractable situation of finding highly numerous local maxima for the fitting surface with truly chaotic processes, one should not give up on the simpler methods unless convinced of their futility in a given setting.

Continuous time problems offer fewer options for parameter estimation than their discrete time counterparts. If the data are measured at sufficiently close intervals, this should cause no problems, because nonlinear least squares can successfully estimate correctly specified models given adequately measured data. However, with measurements more widely distanced in time, it may be better to consider the situation in terms of a mapping problem, thereby specifying the equations to be estimated in difference form and proceeding with OLS or SUR. Because there exist no firm rules at the current time regarding such situations, experimentation and evaluation of a variety of approaches for any given problem is the best and only way to proceed.

5. WHAT IS A CATASTROPHE?

Catastrophe theory addresses a type of dynamical behavior that is among the most important components of the broad area of nonlinear dynamics. Our modern understanding of catastrophe theory had its genesis in relatively recent work by Thom (1975). Since the mid-1970s, our ability to further generalize and apply the early work on catastrophes has grown significantly, and we are now no longer bound by polynomial representations of such models.

Nearly all early work with catastrophe theory involved the use of polynomial functions. In part, this was an important consequence of the great generality of Thom's findings. Because all sufficiently smooth functions can be expanded using a Taylor series approximation (which leads us to a polynomial representation of the original model), it is possible to analyze the polynomial representation directly (see Saunders, 1980, p. 20). As I explain more fully in the next chapter, early catastrophe theorists took this aspect of generality to an extreme, positing that the dynamic structure of large numbers of social phenomena could be analyzed simply by associating these phenomena with canonical polynomial representations of catastrophes. Now, however, the general field of nonlinear dynamics has matured such that social scientists can analyze the catastrophe potential of their own theory-rich models without having to surrender the algebra of these models to one of the canonical polynomials developed by Thom.

Fundamental to catastrophe theory is the idea of a bifurcation. A *bifurcation* is an event that occurs in the evolution of a dynamic system in which the characteristic behavior of the system is transformed. This occurs when an attractor in the system changes in response to change in the value of a parameter. A catastrophe is one type of bifurcation. The broader framework within which catastrophes are located is called *dynamical bifurcation theory*. Two other categories of behavior within dynamical bifurcation theory are subtle bifurcations and explosive bifurcations. Although the remainder of this monograph deals with catastrophic bifurcations, I introduce the subject by discussing one type of subtle bifurcation, the Hopf bifurcation.

A *Hopf bifurcation* occurs in the Lorenz model (involving the birth of a chaotic orbit) for certain values of the parameter r. When $r > 1$, there are two attracting points and one unstable equilibrium point (the origin). At the value of $r = [s(s + b + 3)]/(s - b - 1)$, the Hopf bifurcation occurs as long as $(s - b - 1) > 0$. (For an explanation of these values, see Sparrow, 1986, p. 113.) This is the bifurcation point for the system, and the parameter

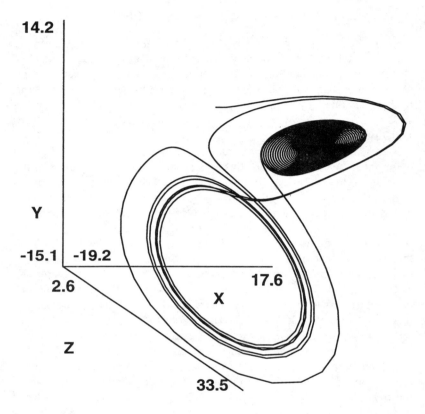

Figure 5.1. The Lorenz System Under Almost (but not Quite) Chaotic Conditions

r is called a *control parameter* because it controls the attracting structure of the system. When the value of *r* is between zero and this value, trajectories eventually fall into a nonrecoverable descent within a basin of one of the attractors. However, when the value of *r* exceeds this value, there is the birth of a permanent chaotic orbit involving two attractors with their basins.

This can be illustrated by choosing a value for *r* that is below, but near, the system's bifurcation value. Figure 5.1 is constructed using the same parameter values as used to construct Figure 2.6, except that the value of *r* is set at 21 instead of 28. (The bifurcation value is approximately 24.74 given the values of *s* and *b* that are used for Figure 2.6.) With significantly lower values for *r*, the trajectory is quickly captured in one of the attracting basins, as is illustrated in Figure 2.5. However, with a value of $r = 21$ as in Figure 5.1, note that the trajectory begins to travel through both of the attracting basins before finally being captured in one of them. For values of r above the bifurcation point, no one basin ever captures the trajectory, and permanent orbital behavior begins.

Subtle bifurcations (such as the Hopf bifurcation) are relatively rare in nonlinear dynamics, in the sense that few examples of such phenomena are known. However, catastrophic bifurcations are very abundant in terms of both mathematical and real-world examples. It is likely that such bifurcations will eventually play a large role in the theoretical development of the social sciences.

As with subtle bifurcations, catastrophes also involve a control parameter. When the value of that parameter is below a bifurcation point, the system is dominated by one attractor. When the value of that parameter is above the bifurcation point, another attractor dominates. Thus the fundamental characteristic of a catastrophe is the sudden disappearance of one attractor and its basin, combined with the dominant emergence of another attractor. Any type of attractor—static, periodic, or chaotic—can be involved in this. Elementary catastrophe theory involves static attractors, such as points. Because multidimensional surfaces can also attract (together with attracting points on these surfaces), we refer to them more generally as *attracting hypersurfaces*, *limit sets*, or simply *attractors*.

In classical catastrophe theory, the various attracting static hypersurfaces are actually connected. However, there are portions of the overall surface that are unstable, and thus repelling. Thus nearby trajectories tend to "fly" quickly past these unstable regions as they move from one stable area to another. It is this relatively rapid snapping movement that is typical of nearly all catastrophe phenomena.

From an algebraic perspective, it is quite simple to create a model with catastrophe potential. To keep things simple, the remainder of my treatment of the subject in this chapter will focus on a catastrophe surface called a *cusp*. The most commonly applied method to create a cusp is to develop a dynamic model that contains a cubed expression of a variable within at least one equation of a system. I postpone discussing substantive reasons for wanting to do this until the next chapter so that I can focus on the mathematical mechanics involved with such models.

Zeeman (1972) developed a model for heartbeats that contains the minimal number of ingredients for a cusp catastrophe. (See also Danby, 1985, pp. 89-94.) Although I need not develop the biological theory here regarding its operation, it is necessary to identify the primary variables involved in the model. In this model, the variable x refers to the muscle fiber length in the heart. The parameter q identifies the overall tension in the system. The parameter A is called a control parameter because it will be used to move trajectories across a catastrophic equilibrium hypersurface. This control parameter refers to the electrochemical activity that is associated with giving the heart instructions regarding when to beat. Thus we need two equations, one to describe change in the variable x and the other to characterize change in the control parameter A. Zeeman's model is

$$\frac{dx}{dt} = -f(x^3 - qx + A) \tag{5.1}$$

$$\frac{dA}{dt} = x - x_1 . \tag{5.2}$$

The parameter f controls the speed of the heart reaction and is ignored in the following discussion because it is of minor substantive consequence to the model. (Numerical experimenters might try values ranging from 1 to 20. Trajectories follow the equilibrium hypersurface more closely with higher values for this parameter.) The variable value x_1 represents the muscle fiber length at systole (the contracted heart equilibrium).

From a mathematical point of view, Equation 5.2 is used simply to change the values of the control parameter A, thereby changing the location of a static point attractor on the larger equilibrium surface as defined by Equation 5.1. To identify the equilibrium surface for the model, it is necessary to set the derivative in Equation 5.1 equal to zero and then to solve for x. Thus we need to solve the equation

$$0 = x^3 - qx + A \tag{5.3}$$

for x given any number of values of the control parameter A. Thus, for example, we are given a value for parameter A, and we must then determine the values for x that will satisfy Equation 5.3 for that value of A. Because parameter q is just an ordinary parameter (i.e., not a control parameter), it is assumed here that its value is estimated elsewhere and subsequently inserted into the equation for analysis. Again, the big difference between an ordinary parameter and a control parameter is that the former has one fixed value whereas the latter changes systematically in a fashion that is determined by the nonlinear system.

If the highest power in Equation 5.3 was squared, we could use the quadratic formula to solve for x, but because the degree of this equation is greater than 2, we need to use some other method. My preference is to use Newton's method for finding the roots of equations. The procedure converges rapidly to the roots, and it is relatively easy to program and efficient computationally. (Programmers should be warned to use a filter and a range of initial conditions with catastrophe models to screen out unsuccessful attempts at convergence.)

Figure 5.2 illustrates the equilibrium surface for Equation 5.3. For this figure, the value for the parameter q was set at 2. This figure has the characteristic S-shape (here in reverse) of the cusp catastrophe. Trajectories can begin anywhere in the phase space, but they are attracted to the surface shown in the figure. Where the trajectories end up on this figure depends on the history of movement for the control parameter A as well as the resting point(s) for this parameter.

Figures 5.3 and 5.4 are constructed using two different values for the parameter q. In each figure, numerous trajectories are given initial conditions and allowed to proceed toward attracting points on the equilibrium surface. The exact same initial conditions are used for the trajectories in both figures. The figures are set up so that there are two equilibria (i.e., resting points) for the control parameter A.

A number of observations can be made when comparing these two figures. The size of the reverse S-shaped equilibrium surface is different for each figure. Also, in Figure 5.3, two points on the surface seem to be attracting equal numbers of the trajectories. However, in Figure 5.4, a point on the upper left portion of the equilibrium surface is more successful at attracting a larger number of the trajectories. Thus the placement of a trajectory's initial condition relative to the equilibrium surface is critical in determining the direction that a trajectory will follow.

Note that in Figure 5.4, some of the trajectories that begin in the lower portion of the figure with positive initial values of the control parameter A move to the left of the figure and then depart from the lip of the equilibrium surface and rapidly (relative to further change in the control parameter) rise upward to arrive at the upper left portion of the surface. This rapid vertical movement coincident with small horizontal displacement is the characteristic feature of catastrophes in phase space. The trajectories, in a sense, snap from one spot on the equilibrium surface to another. The trajectories could not follow the surface past the lower lip because this would have required the control parameter to increase. Thus the middle level of the equilibrium surface is unstable; it actually repels trajectories. Only the

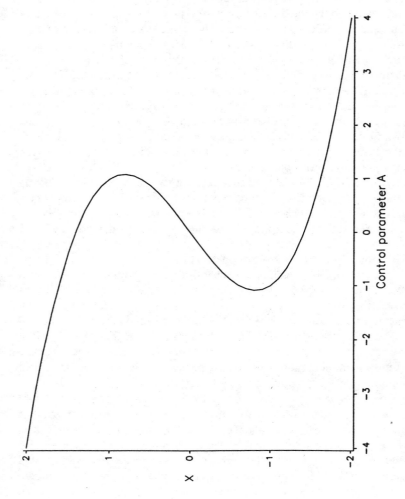

Figure 5.2. A Cross-Section of the Heartbeat Model Catastrophe Equilibrium Surface

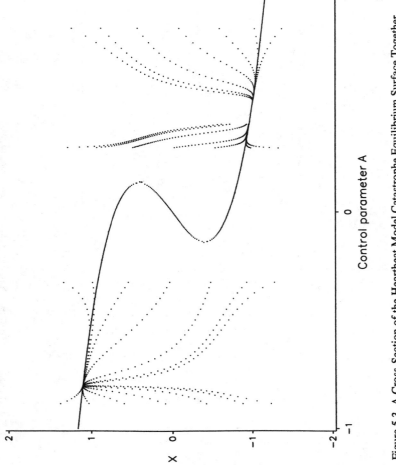

Figure 5.3. A Cross-Section of the Heartbeat Model Catastrophe Equilibrium Surface Together With Variable Trajectories

57

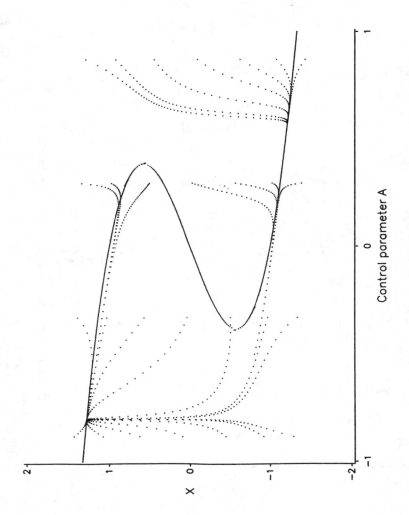

Figure 5.4. An Alternative Cross-Section of the Heartbeat Model Catastrophe Equilibrium Surface: The Basin of One of the Point Attractors Has Increased in Size

upper and lower portions contain potentially stable equilibria for the system. At this point it should be obvious that an endless series of two-dimensional plots could be constructed using any number of values of the parameter q. In modeling catastrophes, it is often useful to create a three-dimensional representation of the equilibria surface using a continuous range of values of such a parameter, thereby identifying how the shape of the surface changes in response to variations in this parameter. This does not make q a control parameter. It is better to think of q as a parameter that can take on any value within a range of values, depending on the substantive context of the problem and as determined by an estimation program. Figure 5.5 is an example of such a graph.

In this figure, the horizontal axis represents the control parameter A, and the other floor axis represents a continuous range of potential values for the parameter q. The three-dimensional shape is that of a cusp, which is why this type of catastrophe is so labeled. Trajectories can travel anywhere in the relevant phase space within which the cusp is located, but they are always attracted to some point on the upper or lower portion of the cusp surface. When trajectories pass over the lip of either of these portions of the surface, they leave the surface momentarily as they relocate to an opposite area on the surface. This results in rapid vertical movement in the phase space of Figure 5.5, substantively implying rapid change in the variable x combined with small changes in the control parameter A, which is, of course, the catastrophe.

Placing the Cusp in the Range of the Data

In the next chapter, I introduce substantive concepts underlying various algebraic approaches to constructing catastrophe models in social scientific settings. However, some aspects of variable scaling are common to all such models, and it is useful to illustrate this now with the current model. To ease the presentation of this topic, I temporarily abandon any of the original substantive meaning underlying Zeeman's heart model, thereby considering it a relatively generic algebraic structure that could have some social scientific meaning. Understand that I do not normally recommend reusing complete models for totally different substantive investigations. That is, indeed, a major source of abuse of the linear model in statistical analyses. I do so now only to illustrate variable scaling techniques using an already familiar model. (One should note that nonlinearists borrow and creatively

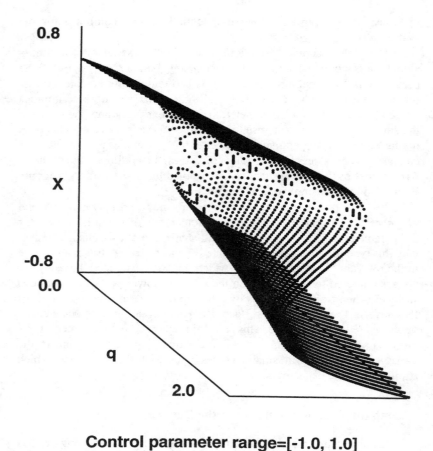

Control parameter range=[-1.0, 1.0]

Figure 5.5. A Three-Dimensional View of the Cusp Catastrophe Equilibrium Surface

recombine in their own models algebraic fragments that are used elsewhere. The end product, however, is usually quite unique to the particular
substantive setting.)

Returning to Equations 5.1 and 5.2, we now assume that this nonlinear
system contains the basic algebra that is addressed in the dynamics of a
theory of interest. Thus we are expecting the equilibrium surface to be a
cusp and that the dynamics of the problem should have catastrophe type

trajectory movements in it. However, the algebra produces this cusp for values of the variable x that are symmetric about zero, and our actual data may be scaled around a different midrange value. Moreover, the range of the values of x in Figure 5.5 is approximately 1.6 (i.e., −0.8 to 0.8). The range of our data may be, say, 100. For illustrative purposes, let us say that our data have a lowest value of zero and a highest value of 100. Thus we need to rescale the algebra of Equations 5.1 and 5.2 so that the cusp can fit into this range.

To begin, we first allow for the vertical shifting. This is done by rewriting the model as in Equations 5.4 and 5.5.

$$\frac{dx}{dt} = -f[(x - v)^3 - q(x - v) + A] \tag{5.4}$$

$$\frac{dA}{dt} = (x - v) - (x_1 - v). \tag{5.5}$$

In these equations, the new parameter v acts to shift the entire activity of the model vertically. A positive value for v moves all model activity upward by exactly that amount.

To widen the range of the now vertically adjusted variable x, we need to include a single multiplier into the algebra. This is done in Equations 5.6 and 5.7 using the parameter m.

$$\frac{dx}{dt} = -f[m(x - v)^3 - qm(x - v) + A] \tag{5.6}$$

$$\frac{dA}{dt} = m(x - v) - m(x_1 - v). \tag{5.7}$$

In practice, of course, the scaling parameters v and m need to be estimated together with all of the other parameters, but it is important to emphasize that these scaling parameters are common features to applications of catastrophe theory in the social sciences. The reason is that the equilibria surfaces associated with catastrophes are the central feature of such models. It makes no sense to use such sophisticated algebraic structures if the complexities of the surfaces cannot appear within the actual range of the data. Rescaling allows the estimation procedure to locate these surfaces properly wherever they may reside in a model's phase space as determined by the data.

To summarize, to allow for the proper placement and scaling of potential equilibria surfaces within the phase space range as defined by the data for a particular variable, subtract a single parameter from each occurrence of the relevant independent variable in the system, then multiply each instance of this now vertically adjusted variable by another parameter. How much of the nonlinear equilibrium surface (e.g., the cusp) actually appears in the data-defined phase space can be determined only after all of the parameters have been estimated.

6. STRATEGIES FOR
SPECIFYING CATASTROPHE MODELS

This chapter suggests theoretical reasons for including algebraic structures that can produce catastrophes within continuous-time models of social processes. The various algebraic specifications presented are not a collection of definitive models from which researchers must borrow for their own work. Rather, this chapter is a collection of ideas, some or many of which may be useful in applied specifications in a variety of contexts. It is unlikely that a researcher would want to borrow an entire model as specified here, but fragments of these models will certainly be useful elsewhere once the principles of application are clearly understood. This chapter also expands the current discussion to illustrate alternative types of catastrophes. To simplify the presentation of material, I do not rescale the variables in the discussions below as is done in the latter part of the previous chapter.

When developing a catastrophe model from first principles, it is important to work from the perspective of social theory, not mathematical theory. Early catastrophe work was heavily criticized for loosely applying general catastrophe models to a wide variety of social processes. Those who made these applications generally drew pictures of cusp type models, labeled the axes to correspond with a specific application, and then proceeded to make broad generalizations. The same pictures (with different labels on the axes) were used to show why a dog barks, why a revolution occurs, why a wave breaks on the ocean, why a person has a nervous breakdown, and so on. Early theoretical work by Thom suggested that all catastrophes could be identified from within a small set of canonical models. The problem in application occurred when theorists took this result too seriously, to the point of avoiding the theory construction enterprise entirely. From the perspective of some observers, the catastrophe theorists had a bag of tricks containing a collection of catastrophe models, and they were loosely associating nearly every phenomenon that contained some element of rapid change with one of these models. This, of course, is one of the primary criticisms made of linear statistical models, that is, the same basic model is used in countless settings, thereby guaranteeing an absolute minimum of isomorphism between theory building and model construction (see Brown, 1995).

Thus my advice to model builders in the social sciences is to think in terms of social processes that might require algebraic structures that could yield catastrophe potential. Build models from an intimate knowledge of these processes while remaining aware of the algebraic requirements for catastrophes. The art of nonlinear model building is a delicate dance with two partners, algebraic forms that produce known effects and a substantive understanding of the complexities of social phenomena. Coordinating the two by mixing structure to match complexity is the job of the theorist, and it is the single greatest creative challenge of any researcher.

The most straightforward way to create a catastrophe model is to develop a model that requires a primary variable that is raised to some power. The simplest of such models is called the *fold*. The requirements for a fold are that the primary variable be squared and that the model contain some other input not involving the primary variable. This other input can be as simple as a control parameter or as complex as a sophisticated nonlinear form. For example, Equation 6.1 produces a fold catastrophe.

$$\frac{\mathrm{d}x}{\mathrm{d}t} = gx^2 + A. \tag{6.1}$$

In this model, g is a constant parameter, but A is a control parameter. As values of the parameter A vary, a catastrophe can be created.

Many types of social process could result in a squared term in a model. For example, Przeworski and Soares (1971) as well as Huckfeldt (1983) propose a variety of nonlinear model specifications for dynamic social and political processes that involve power terms. Often contextual theories involving various forms of information transfer or social interaction involve such specifications. Many other such references, as well as some of my own examples of catastrophe models, can be found in Brown (1995).

The procedures for analyzing Equation 6.1 are the same as those used in the previous chapter for the cusp catastrophe. For a continuous range of values of the parameter A, we are interested in the equilibrium surface for the variable x. Because the variable is squared, there will be at most two values for x for a given value of the control parameter. Thus we begin by setting the derivative (i.e., Equation 6.1) equal to zero and solving for x. One of the roots of the equation will be an attractor, whereas the other will be a repeller (actually, a separatrix). However, there will be other values of the control parameter for which no solution for x exists. At the point at which solutions for x vanish, there is a catastrophe, and the attractor changes from a point on the equilibrium surface to infinity.

Figure 6.1 illustrates a fold catastrophe. Note that for some values of the control parameter, there is an attractor on the parabolic equilibrium surface. But, as the value of the control parameter increases, the separatrix and the

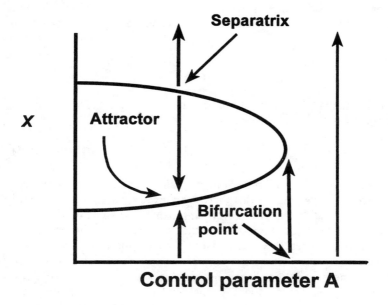

Figure 6.1. The Fold Catastrophe

attractor eventually meet, and this point of intersection is the bifurcation point. Beyond this value of the control parameter, infinity is the system's attractor.

Of course, if the model was written such that what is now the control parameter were changed to be a function, the model would then become

$$\frac{dx}{dt} = gx^2 + A(y), \tag{6.2}$$

where A is now a function of a new variable y (or anything else). Thus the social theorist has complete control over that which controls the appearance of the catastrophe. This is true of all catastrophe models, including the cusp described in the previous chapter. There is no need to restrict the controlling parameter to be a constant. Any level of complexity is allowed in this respect.

Catastrophes also need not rely on polynomial algebra, although this is the most common situation. To understand the variety that is possible in this regard, consider the cusp model discussed in the previous chapter. After setting the derivative equal to zero (repeated here for convenience as Equation 6.3),

$$0 = x^3 - qx + A, \tag{6.3}$$

we can rearrange this to solve for the control parameter, A. This is done in Equation 6.4.

$$A = qx - x^3. \tag{6.4}$$

Figure 6.2 illustrates a graph of this surjective function. The important point to note in this graph is that there is a range of values for the control parameter, A, that can be produced by more than one value of x (i.e., the horizontal line test). It is this ingredient that is necessary for the production of a catastrophe, regardless of how the nonlinear complexity of the model is achieved.

Thus, if one is modeling change in a variable, say dx/dt, almost anything that you do to the primary variable, x, that produces a multivalued response can potentially lead to a catastrophe situation. For example, the following model could produce catastrophes:

$$\frac{dx}{dt} = \frac{\sin(x)}{x} - A. \tag{6.5}$$

The equilibrium surface for this model is illustrated for an example range of values for x and A in Figure 6.3. From this figure it is clear that movement along the axis of the control parameter could produce jumps along the vertical axis as the trajectories leap off of one level at the lip of a curve and are thereby attracted to another level.

Thus one need not be limited by the polynomial algebraic forms developed by Thom. Indeed, one's creativity in response to modeling complex social phenomena is the only real limit, and creativity should ideally have no limit.

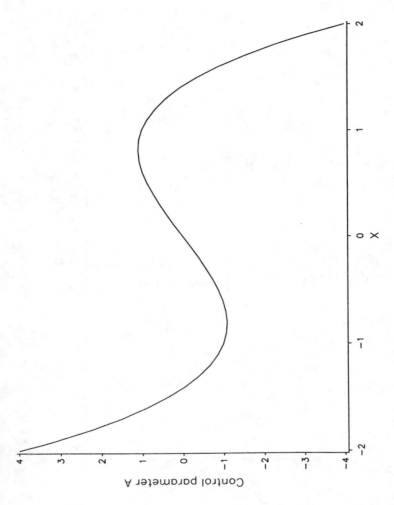

Figure 6.2. Solving for the Control Parameter Identifies the Surjective Nature of the Catastrophe Function on the Variable x

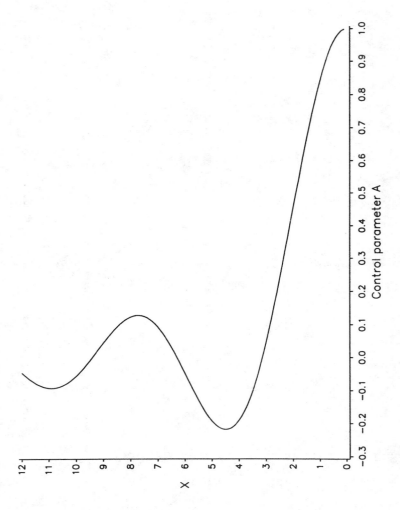

Figure 6.3. A Nonpolynomial Catastrophe Equilibrium Surface

7. ESTIMATING CATASTROPHE MODELS

In a parallel fashion with respect to Chapter 4 for chaotic models, this chapter focuses on matters inherently related to estimating catastrophe models. In situations in which there is one case (e.g., a nation) and many time points, the estimation procedures are no different for catastrophe models from those for chaos models, as described in Chapter 4. Indeed, nonlinear least squares can be quite successful at estimating catastrophe models in such data settings. But adequately long time series of social data are difficult to obtain. Thus, in the social sciences, parameter estimation using catastrophe models typically occurs with respect to data in which there are many cases but few time observations (e.g., many counties or survey respondents but only, say, two time points), and the current discussion focuses on this more common situation.

The basic difference in estimation procedures between the two situations described above is in how the measures of fit are calculated. In the situation in which there is one case and many time points, the residuals between the model's predicted values and the data are calculated and summed after each time period. Beginning with the first initial condition for the system variables, the model is used to calculate the next time period's predicted values. The residuals are calculated with respect to these predicted values and the data. The actual data for this next time period is then used as the model's starting condition for the next time period's value; the residuals are again calculated and summed, and so on. The model's overall fit is based on the correspondence between the predicted values across the entire span of time and the data series.

However, in situations in which there are many cases but, say, only two time points, one has a set of initial and ending points with nothing in between. Thus the data for the first time point are used in the model to predict the next (and the only other) time observation for all cases (see Brown, 1995, Chapter 2). Computationally, this is best accomplished using a matrix language because it is necessary to calculate trajectories for all cases simultaneously, and all observations per time point can be easily organized into a single vector.

In situations in which there are many cases as well as three or more time points, one has a choice of two estimation strategies. Which one to use depends on the individual researcher's theoretical perspective of whether or not the parameters are constant for the system across all time points. If it is determined that the parameters are not constant across all time points, as would often be the case in political settings in which the candidates running in each election are different, then one can simply estimate the model separately for each pair of time points, and nothing is inherently different from the procedures outlined above for two and only two time points. One simply repeats this procedure until the time intervals are exhausted. In practice, because of the time and effort involved with each estimation, this procedure makes sense only in situations in which there are data for only a few (say, three or four) time points.

If more than two time points are involved with the same constant parameters operating in the system across all of the time points, then it is necessary to use the data for the first time point to initiate the estimation procedure in order to predict the value for the second time point. Typically, the actual datum for the second time point, *not* the predicted value based on the first time point, is then used to continue the estimation procedure in order to calculate a predicted value for the third time point, and so on. Residuals are calculated with respect to each predicted value (i.e., the second time point of each pair), summed across cases, and totaled across time.

In all data settings, when calculating the predicted values for the next time point, it is necessary to use a numerical technique such as a Runge-Kutta algorithm across any two time points for all cases. One can expect nonlinearities across time between these two time points, and the degree of nonlinearity is likely to be dependent on characteristics of the data themselves. Thus, to capture these longitudinal nonlinearities, it is necessary to use a sufficient number of iterations of the Runge-Kutta across the two time points to allow for these nonlinearities to materialize. (One iteration with a large step size is identical to differencing, and the longitudinal nonlinearities between the two time points cannot be reconstructed in this way.) My suggestion is to begin by using ten iterations between each pair of time points while using a step size of 0.1. This conveniently divides the time between observations into tenths and allows for sufficient flexibility in graphing routines to produce relatively smooth plots. Smaller step sizes with larger numbers of iterations will further smooth the graphics at the expense of more time being necessary to conduct the estimations.

After projecting the model through, say, ten iterations of a fourth order Runge-Kutta, one then compares the model's ending points with the data for the next time period. The residuals are calculated across all cases (e.g., counties, electoral districts, or survey respondents) and summed. This yields the residual sums of squares needed to calculate the model's fit, as per Equation 4.1. Because the model is supposed to explain the change in the variables between each pair of time points, the total sums of squares needed in Equation 4.1 is calculated from the difference in each pair of temporal data values across all cases, and then summed. It is important to note that one does *not* calculate the total sums of squares from the mean of the later time point.

No prepackaged software currently exists that can perform this nonlinear least squares procedure using data structures similar to those that are common to the social sciences. Although we hope this will change in the future, there is no certainty that this will happen soon. Thus it is currently necessary for researchers to do the programming themselves. Estimation is a critical component of most nonlinear research because in the absence of estimated parameters there are few ways other than simulations to evaluate the suitability of nonlinear models. Simulations can be extraordinarily valuable in certain situations, but when estimation is possible, complete model evaluation is also possible.

I have developed an easily adaptable general program using nonlinear least squares and written in the matrix language of SAS (SAS IML) for estimating nonlinear models with multiple cases and two time points. I have used this program myself to estimate a variety of nonlinear models, including two instances of catastrophe models. The program is included in the appendix of my book *Serpents in the Sand: Essays on the Nonlinear Nature of Politics and Human Destiny* (Brown, 1995). I suggest that some readers who want to start estimating such models might profit by thoroughly studying this program and then adapting it to their own uses. I have had students translate the program into other languages as well, such as Gauss. Moreover, it would not be difficult to adapt the program for multiple time points (i.e., more than two) as well.

To demonstrate the type of results this program is capable of obtaining, I include here a nonlinear model specification, the parameter estimates, and some graphical results that come from an analysis of the fully estimated model. Readers who desire a more detailed presentation in which the substantive reasons underlying the model specification are fully developed should see Brown (1995, Chapter 3). The following model is designed to explain change in feelings toward President Carter during his unsuccessful reelection bid in 1980.

$$\frac{dR}{dt} = p_1 + (p_2 R) \tag{7.1}$$

$$\frac{dL}{dt} = p_3 + (p_4 L) \tag{7.2}$$

$$\frac{dC}{dt} = p_8 [p_5(p_9 + W_2)(1 - p_{10}W_2)(C - p_6) - (C - p_6)^3 + p_7W_1 - C]$$
$$(7.3)$$

where

$$W_2 = (R + L)/2 \tag{7.4}$$

$$W_1 = (1 + L - R)/2 \tag{7.5}$$

This model was evaluated using survey data taken during the 1980 presidential election in the United States. In terms of the variables in the model, R represents feelings for Ronald Reagan, L stands for feelings for the Democratic Party, and C identifies feelings for the incumbent president, Jimmy Carter. The model is a highly nonlinear interdependent system of equations, with catastrophe potential built into the equation for change in feelings for Carter (i.e., Equation 7.3).

There are ten parameters in this model. Because none of the values of these parameters is known a priori, all of these values need to be estimated. Using the nonlinear least squares program mentioned above, I estimated these parameter values, and I present them here as Table 7.1.

In my own experience, I have found that nonlinearities very often emerge as contextually dependent phenomena. For example, things may seem fairly linear for a nation but, for certain subgroups of the population, nonlinearities can be extreme. Thus it is often necessary to condition the parameter estimates. This is done by writing each parameter as a linear function of a conditioning variable. If we call this new variable CONDITION, then we write each parameter similarly as $p = p_a + p_b(\text{CONDITION})$. The conditioned parameter estimates for the above model are also presented in Table 7.1, where the conditioning variables are the proportions of the eligible populations in each survey respondent's county of residence that voted for the Democratic presidential candidate or, respectively, the Republican candidate in 1980. These measures reflect the partisan bias in each respondent's surrounding political environment.

Figure 7.1 contains a phase diagram of a cross section of the catastrophe equilibrium surface for this model in a Democratically conditioned environment, and it is visible in this figure as the S-shaped curve. The other curves in the figure are sample trajectories that result from the various initial conditions for the variables (i.e., for feelings for Carter and the Democratic Party with respect to each voter). Each trajectory represents movement for one voter. The catastrophe equilibrium surface was calcu-

TABLE 7.1
Parameter Estimates

Parameters	National Estimates	Chi-Square (df = 1)	Simon F	Democratic Context	Republican Context
p_1	0.26724	177.668	0.26446	-0.014208	0.03741
p_2	-0.38401	84.316	0.30368	-0.030225	-0.00415
p_3	0.19066	2.496	0.21388	-0.019417	0.02407
p_4	-0.38721	3.519	0.62810	0.029381	-0.02916
p_5	5.98186	9.983	0.01546	0.001897	-0.00334
p_6	0.83441	24.372	0.05422	0.008622	-0.04221
p_7	0.88157	95.546	0.17592	0.052890	-0.09321
p_8	0.41774	59.310	0.10373	0.066099	-0.06038
p_9	-0.13497	0.351	0.00916	0.078435	-0.11694
p_{10}	1.24597	23.406	0.63444	0.043908	-0.01458

Equation	National (Unconditioned) Fits	Democratic Fits	Republican Fits
Reagan	0.22963	0.24074	0.24292
Democratic Party	0.28320	0.28387	0.28408
Carter	0.31120	0.31979	0.32424
System Average	0.27468	0.28147	0.28375

lated using Newton's method, whereas the trajectories were calculated using a fourth order Runge-Kutta algorithm. Readers should observe that the trajectories are attracted to a point on the catastrophe equilibrium surface and that their movement through phase space is largely guided by the shape of the equilibrium surface. Note that the dramatic downward movement of many of the trajectories occurs after they have passed the upper lip of the equilibrium cusp.

It is clear from Table 7.1 and Figure 7.1 that catastrophe models can be estimated and evaluated using existing social scientific data sets. Although social scientists have not yet estimated a truly chaotic model using a set of equations and a data set, successful examples of catastrophe specifications do exist, even though they are still relatively rare. Yet, as with all new things, the greatest adventure is with the trying, and both chaotic and catastrophe model specifications are ideal venues within which researchers can extend their own investigations into nonlinear aspects of political and social life.

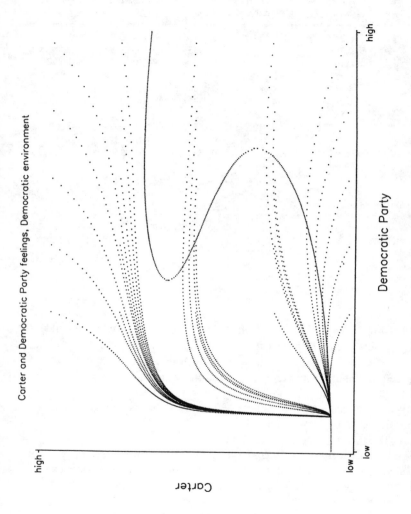

Carter and Democratic Party feelings, Democratic environment

Carter

Democratic Party

high   low   low   high

Figure 7.1. A Fully Estimated Catastrophe Equilibrium Surface Relating Feelings for President Carter and the Democratic Party in a Local Democratic Political Milieu

REFERENCES

BAILEY, N. T. J. (1964) *The Elements of Stochastic Processes.* New York: John Wiley.

BAKER, G. L., and GOLLUB, J. P. (1990) *Chaotic Dynamics: An Introduction.* Cambridge, UK: Cambridge University Press.

BARTLETT, M. S. (1966) *An Introduction to Stochastic Processes.* Cambridge, UK: Cambridge University Press.

BERRY, B. J. L. (1991) *Long-Wave Rhythms in Economic Development and Political Behavior.* Baltimore, MD: The Johns Hopkins University Press.

BROWN, C. (1991) *Ballots of Tumult: A Portrait of Volatility in American Voting.* Ann Arbor: University of Michigan Press.

BROWN, C. (1994) "Politics and the environment: Nonlinear instabilities dominate." *American Political Science Review* 88: 292-303.

BROWN, C. (1995) *Serpents in the Sand: Essays on the Nonlinear Nature of Politics and Human Destiny.* Ann Arbor: University of Michigan Press.

COLEMAN, J. S. (1964) *Introduction to Mathematical Sociology.* New York: Free Press.

CRUTCHFIELD, J. P., and McNAMARA, B. S. (1987) "Equations of motion from a data series." *Complex Systems* 1: 417-452.

DANBY, J. M. A. (1985) *Computing Applications to Differential Equations: Modelling in the Physical and Social Sciences.* Reston, VA: Reston Publishing.

FELLER, W. (1968) *An Introduction to Probability Theory and Its Applications.* New York: John Wiley.

HAMMING, R. W. (1971) *Introduction to Applied Numerical Analysis.* New York: McGraw-Hill.

HAMMING, R. W. (1973) *Numerical Methods for Scientists and Engineers* (2nd ed.). New York: McGraw-Hill.

HUCKFELDT, R. R. (1983) "The social context of political change: Durability, volatility, and social influence." *American Political Science Review* 77: 929-944.

HUCKFELDT, R. R., KOHFELD, C. W., and LIKENS, T. W. (1982) *Dynamic Modeling: An Introduction.* Sage University Paper series on Quantitative Applications in the Social Sciences, 07-027. Beverly Hills, CA: Sage.

KAPLAN, W. (1952) *Advanced Calculus.* Reading, MA: Addison-Wesley.

KAPLAN, W., and LEWIS, D. J. (1970) *Calculus and Linear Algebra, Volume I.* New York: John Wiley.

KING, G. (1989) *Unifying Political Methodology: The Likelihood Theory of Statistical Inference.* Cambridge, UK: Cambridge University Press.

LORENZ, E. N. (1963) "Deterministic non-periodic flow." *Journal of Atmospheric Science* 20: 130-141.

MAY, R. M. (1974) *Stability and Complexity in Model Ecosystems.* Princeton, NJ: Princeton University Press.

MAY, R. M. (1976) "Simple mathematical models with very complicated dynamics." *Nature* 26: 459-467.

76

McBURNETT, M. (1994) *Estimation of Parameters in Chaotic Systems: One and Two Dimensions*. Preliminary conference paper and private communication. Department of Political Science, University of Illinois, Urbana.

McBURNETT, M. (in press-a) "Order and complexity in the evolution of public opinion." In L. D. Kiel and E. Elliot (Eds.), *Chaos Theory in the Social Sciences: Foundations and Applications*. Ann Arbor: University of Michigan Press.

McBURNETT, M. (in press-b) "Probing the underlying structure in dynamical systems: An introduction to spectral analysis." In L. D. Kiel and E. Elliot (Eds.), *Chaos Theory in the Social Sciences: Foundations and Applications*. Ann Arbor: University of Michigan Press.

MEES, A. (1992) "Tesselations and dynamical systems." In M. Casdagli and S. Eubank (Eds.), *Nonlinear Modeling and Forecasting* (pp. 3-25). Redwood City, CA: Addison-Wesley.

MESTERTON-GIBBONS, M. (1989) *A Concrete Approach to Mathematical Modeling*. New York: Addison-Wesley.

MURRAY, W. (1972) *Numerical Methods for Unconstrained Optimization*. New York: Academic Press.

PACKARD, N. H., CRUTCHFIELD, J. P., FARMER, J. D., and SHAW, R. S. (1980) "Geometry from a time series." *Physics Review of Letters* 45: 712-716.

PRZEWORSKI, A., and SOARES, G. A. D. (1971) "Theories in search of a curve: A contextual interpretation of Left vote." *American Political Science Review* 65: 51-65.

PRZEWORSKI, A., and SPRAGUE, J. (1986) *Paper Stones: A History of Electoral Socialism*. Chicago: University of Chicago Press.

RICHARDS, D. (1992) "Spatial correlation test for chaotic dynamics in political science." *American Journal of Political Science* 36: 1047-1069.

SAUNDERS, P. T. (1980) *An Introduction to Catastrophe Theory*. New York: Cambridge University Press.

SPARROW, C. (1986) "The Lorenz equations." In A. V. Holden (Ed.), *Chaos* (pp. 111-134). Princeton, NJ: Princeton University Press.

STIMSON, J. A. (1991) *Public Opinion in America: Moods, Cycles, and Swings*. Boulder, CO: Westview.

TAKENS, F. (1981) "Detecting strange attractors in turbulence." In D. A. Rand and L-S. Young (Eds.), *Lecture Notes in Mathematics 898* (pp. 48-64). Berlin: Springer-Verlag.

THOM, R. (1975) *Structural Stability and Morphogenesis*. Reading, MA: W. A. Benjamin.

WOLF, A. (1986) "Quantifying chaos with Lyapunov exponent." In A. V. Holden (Ed.), *Chaos* (pp. 273-290). Princeton, NJ: Princeton University Press.

WOLF, A., SWIFT, J. B., SWINNEY, H. L., and VASTANO, J. A. (1985) "Determining Lapunov exponents from a time series." *Physica* 16-D: 285-317.

ZEEMAN, E. C. (1972) "Differential equations for the heartbeat and nerve impulse." In C. H. Waddington (Ed.), *Towards a Theoretical Biology* (Vol. 4, pp. 8-67). Chicago: Edinburgh University Press.

ABOUT THE AUTHOR

COURTNEY BROWN is an Associate Professor of political science at Emory University in Atlanta, Georgia. His academic specializations include nonlinear mathematical modeling of social phenomena, politics and the environment, democracy in developing societies, and public opinion and mass behavior. Two other books by the author utilizing nonlinear mathematical approaches to social science problems are *Serpents in the Sand: Essays on the Nonlinear Nature of Politics and Human Destiny* and *Ballots of Tumult: A Portrait of Volatility in American Voting.*

Quantitative Applications in the Social Sciences

A SAGE UNIVERSITY PAPERS SERIES

Other volumes in this series listed on back cover

Quantitative Applications
in the Social Sciences

A SAGE UNIVERSITY PAPERS SERIES

$9.75 each

SAGE PUBLICATIONS, INC.
P.O. BOX 5084
THOUSAND OAKS, CALIFORNIA 91359-9924

Place
Stamp
here